UNRAVELED

BREAK FREE FROM PAIN & HEAL YOUR HEART

ANNIE CALLAHAN

© 2024 by Annie Callahan

Published by Ink & Scroll Press LLC
P.O. Box 1655, Gunnison, CO 81230
inkandscrollpress.com

Printed in the United States of America

All rights reserved. No part of this publication may be reproduced, stored, or transmitted in any form or by any means—whether electronic, photocopy, recording—without prior written permission. The one exception would be brief quotations in printed reviews.

ISBN 979-8-9913398-0-3

Unless otherwise indicated, all Scripture quotations are taken from the Holy Bible, New Living Translation, copyright © 1996, 2004, 2015 by Tyndale House Foundation. Used by permission of Tyndale House Publishers, Inc., Carol Stream, Illinois 60188. All rights reserved.

Scriptures marked AMP are taken from the Amplified Bible, Copyright © 2015 by The Lockman Foundation. All rights reserved.

Scriptures marked AMPC are taken from the Amplified Bible, Classic Edition, Copyright © 1954, 1958, 1962, 1964, 1965, 1987 by The Lockman Foundation. All rights reserved.

Scriptures marked NIV are taken from the Holy Bible, New International Version®, NIV® Copyright ©1973, 1978, 1984, 2011 by Biblica, Inc.® Used by permission. All rights reserved worldwide.

Scriptures marked NKJV are taken from the New King James Version®. Copyright © 1982 by Thomas Nelson. Used by permission. All rights reserved.

Scriptures marked TPT are taken from The Passion Translation®. Copyright © 2017, 2018, 2020 by Passion & Fire Ministries, Inc. Used by permission. All rights reserved. ThePassionTranslation.com.

Some names and details have been changed to protect the privacy of the individuals.

Cover and layout design by Paper & Charm LLC

But now, O Jacob, listen to the LORD who created you. O Israel, the one who formed you says, "Do not be afraid, for I have ransomed you. I have called you by name; you are mine. When you go through deep waters, I will be with you. When you go through rivers of difficulty, you will not drown. When you walk through the fire of oppression, you will not be burned up; the flames will not consume you."
Isaiah 43:1–2

CONTENTS

Part One: Becoming Undone

1. The Undoing 3

2. Life Unraveling 6

3. Lost Hearts 10

4. Tension in Belief 17

5. What Love Is Made Of 22

6. The Weapons We Love With 26

7. The Battle for Your Future 35

8. Dusty Trails and Messy Rivers 41

9. The Reasons We Stay Broken 46

Part Two: Becoming Unstuck

10. The Reality of Being Stuck 54

11. How Stories Are Written 60

12. At the Crossroads 70

13. Purpose in the Pain 78

14. "Why, God?" 86

15. Overcoming Doubt..92

16. Emotions Are Good..99

17. Being Human 106

Part Three: Becoming Unraveled

18. Light & Water 114

19. Calming Storms 119

20. Moving Mountains..125

21. ROAD CLOSED..131

22. Coffee Cups 138

23. Fire Forged..143

24. The *F* Word: Forgiveness 153

25. "Did You Learn to Love?" 163

Notes

About the Author

becoming undone

to be without hope for the future, having experienced great disappointment, loss of money, etc.[1]

becoming unstuck

to no longer be stuck[2]

to be released from being glued, fastened, or bound[3]

becoming unraveled

to be disengaged or disentangled

to come apart by, or as if by separating the threads of

to have the intricacy, complexity, or obscurity of resolved: to be cleared up[4]

PART ONE

becoming undone

to be without hope for the future, having experienced great disappointment, loss of money, etc.[1]

- ONE -
The Undoing

The silence was no longer quiet. A rumbling deep below the surface of our marriage was about to erupt and change everything.

I wanted to shout *ENOUGH!* Cranky kids, dinner burning, the washing machine screeching out a spin cycle, and people waiting on me to push a project through at work. It all felt so overwhelming. But these things weren't the problem. There was an ache in my heart that I couldn't shake, and it was getting harder to silence.

I buried my head in a pillow and screamed, *or* I lashed out at those around me, sending them running in terror. I wanted to tap out, to make it all stop, so I could gather my thoughts, settle back into my heart, and connect to peace.

Even as the world quieted around me, the noise in my mind amplified, becoming a deafening feedback loop I couldn't escape.

Voices echoed through my soul like a wrong note in a favorite song. I sensed that if I wasn't diligent for even a moment, the broken pieces of life would engulf me in waves of pain forever. I wasn't even quite sure what was wrong, but felt the dissonance saturating my entire being.

My solution was to move more, work harder, volunteer, serve, and create—anything to quiet the warnings. I wanted distractions to numb my anxious heart. This strategy worked during the day. At night the fears and thoughts flooded my mind, leaving me exhausted each morning. The disconnection between my husband and me was tangible and terrifying. I tried so hard to ignore the growing uneasiness I was feeling. Too afraid to face the reality of what I knew was going on. *Should I check his phone? No, that would be distrustful.*

Dissonance Within, Distractions Without

Some coping mechanisms are healthier than others, but they are still just coping. The dissonance within was not interested in my external distractions. My heart was screaming, *Can we talk about this? I'm not okay!* The internal pressure multiplied, leaving me with blinding migraines.

Imprisoned in the eye of a hurricane, while calling it peace. I held desperately to an appearance of control and calm, knowing that just one misstep could hurl me through the sharp icicles of a storm I might not survive. I might shatter into a million pieces.

You might be reading this book because someone's pain broke your heart. Or because your broken heart is causing those you love pain. In reality, it is both. We have all been hurt and are hurting, and our pain is spilling onto those around us. It's time to stop the painful cycles.

> ***We have all been hurt and are hurting, and our pain is spilling onto those around us. It's time to stop the painful cycles.***

Our silent screams when life is painful or just overwhelming show up as Netflix marathons, podcasts, or music to replace the intrusive thoughts. Alcohol, drugs, or sex addictions lull us to sleep at night. We pursue excessive fitness routines until the pain in our bodies outcries the pain in our hearts. Or we follow a strict religious duty that promises protection. Or we jump from relationship to relationship, looking for someone to rescue us. These distractions don't always look destructive to those around us. Our partnership with any substance or activity to calm and quiet our hurting hearts is an attempt to manage the storm and feel better, to find peace.

When we refuse to look directly into our own brokenness and confront it, we risk sabotaging the best of what our life could be. I avoided addressing the pain I saw rising in my most intimate partner. I did not have the courage to break the silence and risk more pain. So I kept quiet, prayed, and distracted myself from the reality of the downward spiral we were on. I was too afraid to confront the truth. So, the truth confronted me. Eventually, all things are made known, and this was a head-on collision that left me reeling.

I See You . . .

I look around our world, so beautiful yet broken, and know that you, too, have likely encountered a depth of pain that left you grasping for hope. I have gone to places I never want to be again to provide a lifeline for you. It is possible to stop managing brokenness, and start healing. It is possible to rise above the storm swirling inside you, with hope and peace. It is possible to overcome.

In this book, I offer you the tools that helped me begin to heal and live the *abundant, whole, and free life* Jesus offers, despite pain and suffering. His freedom and wholeness are waiting for you! The evil, broken, and unfair circumstances swirling around you want to destroy your faith and take you out of Jesus' best for you. A rescue mission is underway. Are you ready to rescue *you*? The whole, authentic *you* that longs to show up fully and unapologetically? You are needed, and it is time to be free.

I see you, warrior. Let's move some mountains!

- TWO -
Life Unraveling

Pain came knocking at my door just a few short years ago. While this isn't the only pain I have faced or will face in this life, it left a permanent mark.

My husband had just wrapped up his season of traveling for work, and I was looking forward to a time to connect and rest from the whirlwind. Something wasn't right. It hadn't been right for a long time. He wasn't okay. We weren't okay. I knew why, and I didn't want to know. The pain had begun to seep in years earlier. Or rather, it began to seep *out* as neither of us had faced our internal struggles with identity, rejection, and people-pleasing, just to name a few.

Disconnection and discontent had grown in the darkness. I envisioned that as his winter travel season ended, we would be able to reconnect, plan, and dream about our future. Instead of breathtaking moments, I found myself gasping for air.

It was March 2020. We were planning a birthday party for our youngest daughter the day after Duncan returned from his last and longest trip of the season. He made one of the last flights out of New York, arriving back in Colorado just before travel was shut down for Covid. Our friends and family didn't feel comfortable joining us for the party we had planned, as fear of the pandemic was growing around the globe.

It was a surprisingly sunny March day, and we enjoyed much of it out outside chatting and playing. The girls and I worked on a birthday cake with rainbow frosting and lots of fresh blueberries as decorations. I did a short spin on my bike on the nearby trails and felt full and content with our life. It had been a tough year. I attributed it to my growing business, more work at the church, and the expanding extracurricular activities of our two young daughters. I felt hopeful that everything was going to be okay now. Duncan was home. We were celebrating a birthday. We had made it through a hard season, and now spring was around the corner, and with it, new hope and life.

Friends dropped gifts off on our porch for the birthday girl throughout the day, and we had a cozy family birthday celebration that evening. Dinner, baths, and tucking the girls in for the night. Shew! Another day. And I wasn't doing it alone, as I had so many nights in the past few months.

Shattering into a Million Pieces

My husband and I ended up on the couch, as we had many times before. I had propped my feet up for a foot rub and a chat, when the man I had been with for thirteen years confessed to an affair with another woman.

I recoiled at his hand on my foot. My heart shattering into a million pieces. It hurt to breathe, the shards cut so deep. I had not known pain could cut so deep. The kind of pain that feels too big to carry, threatening to rip you apart, yet you don't die. I am still unraveling the impact of his choices on my heart. Instead of dreaming about our future, I awoke to a nightmare, wondering if there would be a future. Fears, doubts, anger, and suspicions began to crash around me.

There is a Scripture that preaches great, but is brutal to live by: "Dear brothers and sisters, when troubles of any kind come your way, consider it an opportunity for great joy" (James 1:2). Joy was not my first thought. I grieved. I was angry. It hurt like hell. I leaned into God with every last bit of strength I had. In the following days, weeks, and months, I prayed, forgave, repented, and fought with and for Duncan, our marriage, and our family.

I was in a nightmare that I couldn't escape. There was no awakening to a better reality. I barely slept. A flood of pain and sobbing met me each morning. There was only one day, one step at a time. Be present for our two girls, or try my best to be. Make a meal. Do laundry. Get work done. More hard conversations. One brutal, blind step into the unknown at a time.

The Only Way Forward

Life can be hard and broken. The world is full of hurting people—living, breathing, broken pieces of hearts walking around, cutting those who get too close. *Don't let my heart become hard!* I cried out to God. *Help me love and trust again.* I knew this was the only way forward, no matter the outcome of our marriage.

> *Don't let my heart become hard! Help me love and trust again.*

Life-altering pain and loss leave us all with a choice. How will we move forward? Can we move forward? What is life going to be like after this? I have found that following Jesus is not an exemption from pain. How do we navigate brokenness? How do we find the hope God promises us in suffering?

By all accounts, it looked as though our marriage was over. Duncan had already convinced himself that his actions had ended our marriage, and he had no desire or hope for our healing together.

I had a choice: Would I fight for my heart and his, or walk away? I chose to fight for our marriage and, more importantly, for a heart that could learn to trust and love again, no matter the outcome. My goal in telling you our story is to reveal the wounds I found hiding in my heart that had to be healed. To shine a light on the lies we all must overcome when life is painful.

I pressed into the process of healing and forgiveness. I chose love. I confronted anger. I grieved deeply. God was there in it all, speaking to me, holding me, and healing me. There seemed to be no way out of the crushing weight of this hell. But God. When I felt myself slipping under the waves of this storm, His strong hand didn't allow me to go under. It felt as though I would not survive this storm. It was just too painful. Yet, by God's goodness, I did.

- THREE -
Lost Hearts

I could feel my heart hardening as I navigated this new territory. This was unacceptable. If I allowed myself to go to a place of cynicism and bitterness, I would lose myself and my ability to love and be loved the way I longed for. The words of Jesus echoed in my soul: "Sin will be rampant everywhere, and the love of many will grow cold. But the one who endures to the end will be saved" (Matthew 24:12–13).

Sin is our broken life without Jesus. It creates broken relationships and broken hearts. It steals the best from us, while promising happiness and freedom. We try to fix the brokenness without Jesus, only creating more pain. Hearts that were once tender become cold and impenetrable.

I could not let my heart become brittle or cold by turning inward to protect myself from more pain. I had to figure out how to choose to give and receive love every day.

Jesus' words "the love of many will grow cold" have resonated in my soul since childhood. *How terrible!* I thought. *How could someone not love?!* Yet here I am, decades later, more aware than ever of the battlefield we must all step onto to protect and preserve love for self, others, and God. Love is

God's essence and is the currency available freely to all who accept it. Without God, we do not have love. In this season, I knew I needed to do whatever it took to keep my heart close to God. That meant learning to love again after the icy waves had pierced my heart.

We all face things that are just plain hard. People hurt us, circumstances seem against us at every turn, and door after door closes before us. Life doesn't always play fair. We get bumped, bruised, and pushed aside by people navigating their journeys. Our mistakes, and those of others, cost us deeply.

During these seasons, a dark temptation threatens to rob us of all that is good. And if the circumstances weren't hard enough, more is at stake than meets the eye. When people act horribly and the situation is more than we can handle, we are faced with destructive choices to do whatever it takes to feel better.

The real threat in these moments is that we could lose our hearts—our core of hope and love. Sneaking in through the back door as we process pain are familiar but deadly attitudes such as unforgiveness, anger, jealousy, resentment, gossip, and comparison. These are only temporary solutions to feel better in a moment. Ultimately, choosing temporary, pain-numbing solutions limits our opportunity for real healing. The solutions pain presents us with can seem rational and even healthy. However, agreements with self-protection invite a partnership with darkness and isolation, resulting in bondage, not freedom. A thought or belief that points toward self as the solution to our pain is dangerous to our hearts.

Betrayal revealed unhealthy habits and destructive lies in me that I had ignored for far too long. When we are hurting, we are vulnerable to great deception. When we don't have hope and are desperate to feel better, we will take the bait of self every time. The collateral damage to those who love us is not inconsequential.

The root of these thoughts is not discernment or wisdom, but jealousy, comparison, and suspicion. These are agreements we are tempted to make in the wake of loss, disappointment, and pain. Jesus offers us the power to overcome these lies.

While major, life-altering "Big T" traumas are where these temptations are most noticeable, we are just as susceptible to partnering with these agreements in minor ways as well, one disappointment, one failed project, and one fight with our spouse at a time.

When offered a weapon of darkness to protect our hearts, we must recognize it as a trap. The promise of an escape from pain won't lead us to freedom. Jesus doesn't offer an escape; He promises to walk through the pain with us until we are free and whole.

Choosing Not to Lose Heart

In the face of betrayal, I knew I couldn't let unhealthy thoughts and mindsets take root in my heart. Partnering with such lies is devastating; they steal our connection to Jesus. Not all at once. Little by little, as our heart leans away from Him and His love, into self-protection.

These responses are so common that it's easy to believe they are benign. They are anything but. These mindsets create malignant conditions that our hearts cannot survive. Untold damage to our souls will result if we don't address these agreements head on. The solution? Turn toward God's love, allowing Him to heal the pain and free us from the temptation of self-protection.

Paul writes this encouragement to the church in Corinth: "Therefore we do not lose heart. Though outwardly we are wasting away, yet inwardly we are being renewed day by day" (2 Corinthians 4:16 NIV).

The Greek word Paul chose for *lose heart* is *ekkakeō*. It is defined as "to lack courage, lose heart, be fainthearted, or to grow weary."[1] Looking around our culture today, it seems many have lost their hearts and courage. Jesus encourages us to overcome this world and the strategies of evil. But all we often want to do is curl up in the latest comfort or distraction.

In another letter, this time to his friends in Ephesus, Paul uses this same word: "So please don't lose heart because of my trials here. I am suffering for you, so you should feel honored" (Ephesians 3:12–13).

I notice something in both of Paul's statements. Even though outward circumstances cause us to feel beaten down, our hearts can be strengthened and filled with courage every day. We choose the way of Jesus, even when it doesn't make sense. In betrayal I was angry, hurt, and afraid. I had to fight not to allow rage, slander, or evil toward others to take over my heart. Allowing the weariness of pain to overcome my soul would cost me more than I could pay.

Paul continues his letter with, "Get rid of all bitterness, rage, anger, harsh words, and slander, as well as all types of evil behavior. Instead, be kind to each other, tenderhearted, forgiving one another, just as God through Christ has forgiven you" (Ephesians 4:31–32).

Practically, overcoming consists of every small, seemingly unimportant decision to choose Jesus' way of life instead of yielding to self-protection. Every decision toward forgiveness, love, truthfulness, and integrity keeps our hearts open and pure before Jesus. Every decision away from following Jesus' way of life hardens us just a bit more, until we have closed His voice out entirely. When we lose the courage to do what is good and right, we miss the second part of Paul's revelation that we are *renewed and brought to life inwardly*.

I have seen many choose self over love and even justify it biblically, revealing how desperately hard their hearts had become. The world needs us to wake up, find our courage, and allow Jesus to breathe love into our hearts again. What if we choose Jesus over the comfort of protecting our mistakes or hiding our rebellion to His ways? Life will leave us bruised and broken. We must make the decision to renounce the ways of self that keep us fragmented, and we must turn to Jesus, following His way to healing.

> ***The world needs us to wake up, find our courage, and allow Jesus to breathe love into our hearts again.***

Escaping into self-protection leaves us imprisoned in a contract with darkness. Hiding in the dark is not freedom. Solutions offered to us in pain that are void of love for ourselves and others are counterfeits to true healing.

Rage and anger are false forms of power making us feel safe, in control, heard and seen, if only for a moment. Unforgiveness promises to protect us from being harmed again. For some, it's alcohol, drugs, or sexual encounters that promise to soothe the anxiety and fear growing in the darkness. Yet those only leave us more bound to find another fix. Those types of agreements leave our hearts as closed, hardened vessels that cannot give or receive love.

We must hold our hearts gently as light and love reveal our wounds and shadows. Life will be hard and unfair. Bringing a broken heart to Jesus reveals and heals the infections threatening to poison us.

The name of Jesus is the weapon that shatters darkness. When we walk into a dark room, we find the light switch. When we find our hearts enveloped in darkness, we can declare *Jesus* and the darkness must flee. A hundred times in my journey to healing, the only prayer I could utter was *Jesus, help me*. He turned on the light of hope to a life beyond pain. He brought peace and walked with me through another moment, another day. He will walk with you, too, and help you break every agreement you've made to protect yourself. He will reveal Himself to you as a shield and protector in every circumstance, failure, and sadness of life.

Stumbling in the Dark

It wasn't enough that I find my way out of this darkness; I wanted to do all that I could to help Duncan find his way out also. I knew this man, and I knew his heart. He was a good man, and he was hurting. In darkness we rage against those trying to love us. Pain does not play fair.

The stakes were high, and this was where I got to put to the test everything that I said I believed.

When we first met, Duncan was finishing up his college degree and had been an athlete since high school. Months before we married, he casually stated that there was this race he wanted to do later that fall, *just one time*, to *get it out of his system*. The Leadville Trail 100 is a 100-mile race that begins at 10,000 feet in the Colorado mountains. Duncan placed well that year, won it the next, and seven years later he was still running competitively.

Until he wasn't. A strict diet and training regimen, plus a growing family and a new career as the head of a university department, took its toll on his body, and his soul. Trying to do what he loved while building a career, managing a team, providing for his family, and never feeling as if he could get ahead in any area had caught up to him.

I remember the night he told me that he felt as if a black cloud had descended on him. Depression? Hopelessness? I didn't know what to do with that. Neither of us did. I'm sure I rattled off some cliché, and more damaging than helpful Christian rhetoric about praising God and remembering to be thankful. Duncan didn't need tools; he needed hope. Darkness doesn't care about your disciplines; it must be addressed with faith on the battlefield.

I did all that I knew to do—keep the house clean, keep the kids fed and on time to school and activities, trying to hold us all together. Meanwhile I was building a business and growing my capacity in other areas of teaching and leading Bible studies. I would stay up until 1:00 a.m. so many nights, getting work done for my clients. In my heart, I knew I should go to bed with my husband. But there was just so much to do. And I was afraid. Duncan was so cold, and distant. What if I was rejected? The days were a fog of more work, chores, and kid duties. More and more, I felt like a single mom.

We both dove into more work. Unaddressed burnout and depression, masked with productivity and a growing disconnection in our marriage, fueled the hopelessness settling deep into Duncan's heart. A storm was raging on the horizon as we rowed our leaky boat feverishly, pretending the storm wasn't swirling around us.

- FOUR -
Tension in Belief

I believe in forgiveness. I believe that hearts can heal. I believe that people can choose life. I believe that there is nothing God cannot redeem or restore. *But now what?* I wasn't sure I had what it would take to fight this battle. I also have the gift of *too stupid to quit*, and a family and marriage worth fighting for.

I was strung tightly between what I believed, what I could choose, and my husband telling me he was done, explaining what his next steps, *without me*, were going to be.

I tell you our story to show you the gravity of the battle we were in—the battle we all are in. You and I have an enemy who wants to destroy everything good, and we must know the strategies laid out against us if we are to overcome. And we can overcome! We are well-equipped warriors fighting for love.

Healing takes awareness and intentionality, not just to see what's going on in our own heart and mind, but to address it. It sounds crazy to relive what has hurt us, and to allow the tears to flow again. We work so hard to turn off the gnawing questions and the unresolved ache. I reached a point where more talking wasn't bringing healing. I was done hashing out the past; I needed real freedom. At one point, I wrote in my journal,

> *There is peace. Even hope. But also there is a pain that I cannot shake. A deep, bleeding wound that won't get better. I am out of tears. I feel frozen, numb. But not quite. Will there ever be a time where this does not torment me? God, help. Thank you that your presence can heal all. That your goodness can work this into something beautiful.*

Questions left unanswered do not remain silent. Closing our heart off with a declaration of *no one will ever hurt me again* does not keep us from pain. Wounds do not heal through neglect. They remain—screaming to be resolved.

But there is an answer to our questions, and a Healer to address these wounds. To find the answer, we must feel again. More importantly, we must trust again. Opening our heart, if even just a crack, to let in a sliver of light. The scar tissue must be broken up so that new, tender flesh can be uncovered. But will we allow this process?

Love Duncan. Trust Me.

God spoke so clearly to me as I desperately wanted to shut out everyone and everything. When I was finding my footing in the wreckage and unsure whom or what to trust, God said, *Love Duncan. Trust Me.*

I could do that. I didn't have to trust Duncan. Yet. I could trust God to show me the way forward. I could trust Him for a good future. I learned to trust that God held my heart and wouldn't let me stay in this place of pain. When fear raged and I was so scared to move toward Duncan, I reminded myself that God was faithful and wouldn't let me fall. I could be betrayed, rejected, and divorced, yet know that God was at work, no matter what, to create a beautiful future for me. I learned the value of choosing to fight for love, and to resist fear, no matter the circumstance.

We ask so many questions when we are hurting. The answer I found is Jesus. His presence. No one else, nowhere else. To find freedom, to overcome pain and suffering, we must allow Jesus to touch our hearts, and deeply.

> *To find freedom, to overcome pain and suffering, we must allow Jesus to touch our hearts, and deeply.*

I get it—this is hard. You and I . . . we have stuffed and packaged and bandaged and spiritualized our mess. Carefully crafting our life to keep anyone, ever, from getting close again. Even God. Maybe especially God. We spin in circles, trying to figure out how, why, who, and what is to blame. These questions don't have answers. They only lead to suspicion and isolation.

I have seen many people turn away from God's love when they're at their darkest and most desperate, and miss the journey to wholeness. Some do it in a moment. Others bit by bit, as they close off their hearts to people. Afraid to trust or love, they lose the courage to show up fully. Ultimately, they lose the awareness of God's presence.

The truth is, we can't shut *others* out and not shut *Him* out.

A Journey of Becoming Undone

Stepping into freedom is a journey of courage and resolve. It's as simple as opening the door to love and being held until we are whole. It's as messy as tears and anger and fear being released. Like rebreaking a bone to set it right, or massaging hard, calloused scar tissue to allow movement again.

Everything in us wants to hold onto what we know. It's ugly, but we know it, and it feels safe. Anger, bitterness, cynicism, and suspicion promise to protect us from more hurt. Instead, they keep us isolated from true life.

Life is a journey of becoming undone. So fully, completely surrendered to God's presence that we willingly relinquish anything that would separate us from Him. In turn, we receive what we have needed most all along: our lost hearts.

These words from Paul encourage us to focus on Jesus and a future He wants to lead us into:

> I focus on this one thing: Forgetting the past and looking forward to what lies ahead, I press on to reach the end of the race and receive the heavenly prize for which God, through Christ Jesus, is calling us. Philippians 3:13–14

When we walk through the trials of life, we have the choice to press forward to encounter Jesus, allowing Him access to the most vulnerable parts of our story. Our journey is about healing from the wounds inflicted on our hearts, until every twisted and knotted thing becomes undone.

You will not find the life and freedom you desire until you surrender your current life to Jesus. In shedding our broken, battered, shame-filled, arrogant, and selfish life, we are filled with new hope, new joy, new dreams, and restored love.

If you are carrying a broken heart, this may be hard to hear: *It's time to fight, not lick your wounds. It's time to rise, not remain beaten down. It's time to trust God, when nothing feels safe.*

This is the way forward, and it is worth every step along the way. You were designed to fight with the strength of heaven and the gift of faith. You are able to wield God's promises to overcome no matter what the trial, held safe by truth and love.

The next section of my journal reads,

> *Please empower me not to give up too early, but to fight in the time and way and with the tools you give me. Please help me choose love. One day at a time. One moment. One choice at a time.*

- FIVE -
What Love Is Made Of

The starting place for moving out of pain is this: *You are loved.*

Tools had been deposited in my soul long before I needed them. God had equipped me for a battle I never wanted to fight, before I ever stepped onto the battlefield. The curriculum centered around being a warrior of love and light, while learning to rest in His love.

This training came as books and podcasts. Happening upon message after message from church leaders, life coaches, and counselors that built into me the relational, emotional, and spiritual tools I was lacking. It seemed as if every podcast, sermon, and book I picked up were all echoing the same themes: how to choose love, set healthy boundaries, speak up when needed, and overcome unhealthy mindsets. I was being transformed into a warrior who could stare down the strategies laid out against me and my family. I had been in boot camp, and I didn't know it.

Simply knowing great principles doesn't win battles. It grieves me to see so many people reduce their lives every time a challenge comes their way. They can quote Scriptures and recite faith-based principles, but they never seem to put these into practice on the battlefield. Battles will come to all our doorsteps. Will we stay safely locked inside great, yet untested and unchallenged theories?

I wish that no one ever had to suffer. But I have also found that when we encounter battles that trespass too close to what matters most, we are left with only one option: to rise up courageously with what has already been placed in our hands and fight back.

Fighting for Love in a Broken World

As I walked through betrayal, I had to remind myself often that I was fighting for love in a broken world. What felt so deeply personal, was not. The cuts that left me bleeding were caused by the brokenness of others. My mission was to learn to walk in love. I had to make the choice to put into action love, trust, and hope every day. Trusting God's love was the foundation of my healing.

God had equipped me for what was coming in advance, and He protected my family. He was with me in the darkest nights. I can see now all of the ways His goodness was being woven into our story. I know He is weaving strength and beauty and love into your story, too. How good and gracious and kind God is, to make a way through every difficulty on our path.

In pain, we face lies about our worthiness, beauty, and strength. Pain can wear down our souls until we lose all hope. The unchanging, undeniable love of God is the weapon we wield to win this battle. God's love is the anchor that will hold us steady in the storm, and the strong arm that will pull us out of the pit. If you have not yet known God to be good, or if you aren't sure if what you've seen in Christians, church, or life is the kind of "love" you even want, please stay with me just a bit longer. People get love wrong all the time. God's love will never wrong you.

As a parent, I want my kids to know how much I love them. Always and forever, no matter what. If there were a way to infuse every part of their sweet bodies and saturate their every thought with the confidence of my love for them, I would.

Is this what God has done for us? Paul, a leader of the early Church, declares, "We know how dearly God loves us, because he has given us the Holy Spirit to fill our hearts with his love" (Romans 5:5).

God has always desired that we know—really know—His saturating, all-encompassing love filling every part of us. Every cell, every thought, every memory, as we turn to Him to be filled and saturated with His love. Love calls us out of the darkest night, out of death. Love whispers victory, even as death beats against our lives. Love holds our very being together when we feel we will be ripped apart.

> ***Love calls us out of the darkest night, out of death. Love whispers victory, even as death beats against our lives.***

Those who have experienced God's love don't shrink back when death is pounding at their door. They rise boldly to love more courageously, release hope-filled prayers, and reach back for others entangled in what they themselves have overcome. Can you hear God's whisper? *This is not the end of your story . . . I am here. Always and forever . . . No matter what . . .*

Anchored by Love

When your heart longs for answers and demands to know if God even cares, look back. What glimmer of hope anchored you in your darkest moments? That was God's love. Where were you protected and provided for when you were at your lowest? God's love covered you. When did you just know where to go, or what to do? God's love was whispering to you. Where do you see Him preparing you, making you strong and courageous for the battle? You can choose to believe in love. Will you?

God initiated a rescue mission for *your heart* before crafting the world. He saw you and loved you before you cried your first tear. He saw the struggles you would face and made a way through for you, before you even got there. He prepared you, protected you, and loved you through it all. He loves you because He made you and you are His. You cannot mess that up.

I long for the day when I meet Jesus face-to-face and can see through His eyes all the ways He was in my darkest moments. When I felt most alone, He was in the loneliness with me. When I was wounded and hurting, Jesus was battered and bruised. Where fear threatened me in the night, choking out all hope and light, Jesus declared, *She is Mine—let her go!*

> We are pressed on every side by troubles, but we are not crushed. We are perplexed, but not driven to despair. We are hunted down, but never abandoned by God. We get knocked down, but we are not destroyed. Through suffering, our bodies continue to share in the death of Jesus so that the life of Jesus may also be seen in our bodies. Corinthians 4:8–10

Such was Paul's experience of God's love as he walked through the worst life could throw at him. As you and I get up and find our way through the wreckage of relational trauma, we see that Jesus not only carried us, but in His own body took the crushing destruction hurled at us.

- SIX -
The Weapons We Love With

It looks pretty on paper to say, "*Just know God's love and everything will be okay.*" We do need to know God's love as the foundation for this journey, but how?

Can you experience real, transforming love from a Being you can't see? Whom you haven't heard clearly from in far too long? Not to mention, Someone you may have doubts about trusting at the moment?

God is good, and He wants the best for everyone. For a lot of people, this is a stretch of the imagination as deep and wide as the Grand Canyon. When we are hurting, it doesn't seem true that a powerful, knowing, loving Being could stand aloof as we endure pain and suffering. I get it. Yet I had seen too much of God's goodness to let my heart doubt Him, or to believe that He really is aloof in our circumstances. I needed to stay anchored in love, even in the middle of my deepest pain.

How did I fight for my heart, and my marriage? I read Scriptures about God's promise to never leave me. Reading through the Psalms gave me peace. The words washed over me, revealing that He is a God who fights with and for me in these battles. Emblazoned on every page, I found His desire to give me a beautiful future and a whole, healed heart. I wrote these promises down, put them in my pocket, taped them on my mirror, and made notes in my phone. Ammunition for every fear and doubt at the ready. I memorized and prayed the promises I found, even declaring the truth in front of a mirror. This is how the truth and beauty of God's love became embedded in my soul.

In this process, I learned that I had some deep issues with Father God. Jesus and I were good, and the Holy Spirit is amazing. But the idea of God as a caring, protective Father who wanted to step in and help me? I "knew" it; I've even preached it. Yet I didn't realize how deeply I struggled with the idea of God stepping into this role for *me*. I have never doubted God's goodness of character or intention. I came to realize that I viewed Father God as an elderly, caring, yet distant and unapproachable Man sitting on His throne, far away from the realities of my everyday life. Good, absolutely . . . But caring? Involved? Probably not.

A few months after Duncan's confession, I signed up for a prayer session focused on healing. I wasn't expecting the leader to go right to the door marked *Annie's Issues With God*. From the very beginning, she started with, "Let's ask God what lies you are believing about Him."

I probably rattled off what I just shared with you. I knew God was good, but He seemed far away and uninvolved in my daily life. Then she asked the question, "How does God want to be in a relationship with you?"

Tears began to flow as I saw and felt myself walking playfully, hand in hand with a younger version of the Man from before. He wasn't feeble; He wasn't sitting, stuck in a big chair. He wasn't too busy and important to come down from His throne of power and authority to be with me. He was fun, and full of life. He even laughed, as He *enjoyed* being with me. This image of God, alongside me, playfully fun and full of life, was a huge breakthrough for me.

Undoing Distorted Images

The men in our lives can distort our image of God. Have you known father figures who were distant, power-seeking, insecure men uninterested in your day-to-day life? You may have known men as abusers of body or soul. Maybe your experience of a father, husband, brother, or leader caused you to believe that God is critical, angry, or only seeking self-promotion.

God's love has the power to wash away the residue of our pain and suffering. The Bible tells us that *God is Love*. If love is the cure for our brokenness and God is the source of love, we must undo the distorted images of God that are keeping us from receiving His real and true love.

In what's known as "The Love Chapter" in the Bible, 1 Corinthians 13, Paul pens beautifully what love is, giving us a glimpse into this Being who is Love:

- Love is patient and kind.
- Love is not jealous or boastful or proud or rude.
- Love does not demand its own way.
- Love is not irritable, and it keeps no record of being wronged.
- Love does not rejoice about injustice but rejoices whenever the truth wins out.
- Love never gives up, never loses faith, is always hopeful, and endures through every circumstance.[1]

How we receive and give love will be the most important part of our life. I like to remind myself of God's nature by replacing *love* with *God* in these verses:

- God is patient and kind.
- God is not jealous or boastful or proud or rude.

- God does not demand His own way.
- God keeps no record of being wronged.
- God rejoices whenever the truth wins out.
- God is faithful, and He never loses faith.
- God always has hope.
- God will never quit or give up on me, whatever I'm going through.

This perspective has helped me heal, and learn to trust God. I cannot wear out God's love. He is not demanding or arrogant. He is faithful, and full of hope for me and my circumstances. His kindness always leads me back to His love.

I will ask you what the prayer session leader asked me that day: "What lies are you believing about God?" And, "How does He want to be in a relationship with you?"

A Spiritual Adjustment

I began to experience migraines that grew in intensity and frequency, leading me to the office of a chiropractor. My previous experience with chiropractors wasn't good, but I was desperate to put an end to the blinding, day-stopping headaches, and someone had suggested that this might help. The chiropractor introduced herself simply as "Mimi."

An adjustment from Mimi feels like being wrapped in a giant mama-bear hug. She wraps her arms around me, positioning her hands on the spot on my back that needs to be repositioned. She gently rocks me side to side, coaxing me to relax. Then, she can make the adjustment. It's not just Mimi's arms, but her presence that makes me feel safe in this rather awkward and intimate process. Her work realigns bones and brings freedom of movement and the release of tension.

Frequently, Mimi would have to tell me, "I don't need your help. I've got you." She would be positioning my limbs or neck where she needed them to go, and I would "help" by moving my body for her. To be clear, if it were humanly possible for me to align my own skeletal system, she wouldn't have had a job. But it's not possible. Mimi knew what she was doing and didn't need me to move my head or arms or legs for her.

During the time I was Mimi's patient, I attended a Global Awakening healing conference in Colorado that hosted Randy Clark and Bill Johnson. Our marriage had become more stable. Duncan was working hard to rebuild trust and love. We had just come out of a spring break trip that was everything I had hoped for the previous spring. Yet I was still hurting so deeply, struggling with fear, suspicion, comparison, grief, anger, shame . . .

At the conference, there was a session focused on ministry and healing. I stayed toward the back where my group was sitting, under the balcony's shadows, near the exit door. As the leaders urged people to come forward for prayer, I stayed frozen to my spot. I was so hungry for emotional healing, but the walk to the front felt too exposing. Even after a year, I was carrying so much shame and humiliation from betrayal.

But God found me. He wasn't concerned with where I was in the building. He heard my heart crying out for freedom and knew exactly why I couldn't walk to the front of the room that night.

I've never experienced God's presence like that before. I was quickly a complete puddle of tears and snot, as waves of God's healing love burned away what I had experienced the year before. I wasn't shedding tears of grief or self-pity. The only way I know how to describe the experience is that it felt as if the Father's love was washing and healing the broken parts of my heart. It was an undoing of death's hold on me.

I remember thinking while sobbing, *What do I need to do? Should I pray?*

Quote Scripture? Worship? I didn't want to miss anything God might want to do. I was so desperate for healing and peace, and I thought somehow I could do something to really get the most out of this encounter in God's presence.

Adorable, right?

God thought so too. In my heart, His message came through loud and clear. In a mama-bear Mimi tone, He stated, *I don't need your help. I've got you.*

I don't need your help. I've got you.

That day, God didn't need me to do anything but show up and trust Him. To relax into His Father-bear hug and let Him adjust and align what was out of place in my soul. I was overwhelmed by His love, His goodness to show up for me, His willingness to heal me.

As the service was wrapping up, Randy Clark and his team came right up the aisle I was in. My group had chosen seats off to one side, in the back, and as close to an exit door as possible. The rest of the weekend, Randy's team had used a side door at the front of the room. Not this time. I had just about pulled myself together to go to dinner with friends when Randy singled me out, placed his hand on me, and said "More!" Which was his way of asking God to fill me with *more* of Himself. I felt another wave of God's love wash over me.

God didn't need me to go to the front that night. He knew that being up front would have been a distraction to me. And He knew I needed assurance that I didn't miss a single thing. He brought Randy Clark to me.

I got one of the best spiritual adjustments of my life that night.

I'm a recovering helper. Maybe you are, too? I still think I can fix my own soul the way I think I can adjust my own body's skeletal alignment. Don't get me wrong—there are things we can do to take great care of our bodies and souls. Yet there are also times when we need the Healer to reveal and heal what we cannot.

God doesn't need our help; He needs our trust and surrender. We get to show up and participate. Allowing His presence to open us up, like a skilled surgeon, cutting away the poisonous infections of past wounds. Another way God often tells me *I don't need your help* is *Be still, and know that I am God!* (Psalm 46:10).

Fighting in Worship

Worship is where God can do His best work in me. I know God's love most when I worship. I am open and surrendered. I can't stay long in God's presence without coming to a crossroads. Will I abandon my heart fully, allowing Him completely and fully to love me? The alternative choice is to go through the motions, feel a little better, and get out of there as quickly as possible.

In intimate worship, God is going to want to talk about the closed doors and hidden fears. He will want to peek in, and He will see the bitterness and offense we're trying to bury. He will want to dig up the shame lodged deep inside, and uproot the insecurities and lies we're tethered to. God wants full, surrendered access—never to hurt us, but to free us.

God reminded me of this promise from the Bible: "The Lord will fight for you, and you shall hold your peace and remain at rest" (Exodus 14:14 AMPC). Worship invites God into our battles, silencing fear and giving us the courage to choose love.

There were many times when worship was a struggle for me. I was wading through so much fear, pain, and brokenness that it felt as if I couldn't bear any more open-heart surgery. I was tired of tears and snot. I was exhausted from weeping. God met me every time with just what I needed. When I could only crack open my heart a sliver, God poured in all the peace and love I could contain. He always provided what I needed, even when I didn't know what I needed. We always have the choice to let God in, or keep our heart locked up tightly. I have never regretted opening my heart to God, even when it meant dealing with what I was afraid to face.

Our temptation is to run from God when life gets hard and we are reeling with questions about His love and goodness. The lie that He isn't good keeps us from pursuing Him in the struggle. Yet we can be honest with Him about our pain, fear, and doubts. Ask Him to show you where He was, and is, in your story. He longs to show you.

If you are ready to encounter God's love, find time and space where you will not be interrupted. A place where you can be still and let God's heart meet yours. You don't need music, but there's so much available, if it helps you. Bring a journal, just in case. Writing helped me get the chaotic thoughts and feelings out of my head, while also inviting God's words, perspectives, and promises to flow through my pen onto the pages.

Allow the tears and fears and pain to bubble to the surface. It's okay! Jesus is there with you. Don't struggle to worship the right way, or say the right things. Let Him lead, and find rest in His presence. He knows what you need, and He knows the path to your freedom.

The storm I walked through helped me find a deeper reality of God. He helped me walk free from things I didn't even know I was bound by. If you dare to walk this out with me, I know you can experience this too.

Life is both beautiful and broken. I may never meet you or hear your story, but I know that you picked up this book, at this time, for a reason. I believe it is time to face the things that shook you to the core and left you feeling irreparable. I'm here to tell you that it is possible to come out of the fire refined, forged, and holy. What was sent to break you can become a beautiful strength. No matter what you're facing, you can love and dance and sing and be comfortable in your own skin again. It is possible.

Whatever your story, I pray that you can hear God declaring over you, *This is not the end of your story* . . .

Actually, it's not even your story. It's His. When your story is told, let it be of God's love wrapping around you and forging a faith so beautiful that nothing could overcome it. Let it be of the redemption and hope that darkness could not extinguish. You can come out of the flames brighter, stronger, and more secure in His love. The moments that left you gasping for air will leave you breathless when you see His goodness interwoven into every scene.

I will leave you with this thought from a friend who walked with me in my journey:

"The things that seem irreparable are not so."

- SEVEN -
The Battle for Your Future

My parents divorced when I was a freshman in high school. It wasn't until several years later that I began to unravel the lies anchored in my soul from their decision. Lies whispering questions like, *Why wasn't I good enough for a healthy, whole family, or for the promotions and opportunities that came so easily to others? Why does my life feel as if I'm trudging through knee-deep mud?*

I have rarely blamed God for difficulties in life, but I have definitely questioned Him. *Why me, God?* Or, *Why not me, God?* Instead of turning on Him, I turned on myself. I figured if God is good, then I must be deficient for life to be so hard.

When we believe that our past failures and other people's actions have disqualified us from God's purposes, then they have. Believing that our struggles are because *we are unqualified or unfit* will stop us from building something beautiful today.

We have an enemy who knows the gifts God has deposited within us. He recognizes the unique ways we were designed to reveal God's love to this world, so he works hard to tarnish and stain every bit of that love. This causes us to doubt how perfectly formed and loved we are by Father God.

Fear, shame, abuse, loneliness, failures, death, and loss don't come knocking at our door because we are bad or broken. Hard things, bad things, and even evil are part of our world. The devil won't hesitate to turn these into weapons to wield against our identity. His strategy is to convince us to undermine our own gifts and lay down our strength. Bold-faced lies cause us to believe that our purpose is lost in the pain of this moment, blinding us to see ourselves as God sees us.

Yet God's declaration over each one of us is a reality that no one can touch or revoke. Resounding before this earth was formed, He had us in mind, preparing ahead of time the good works that each of us could uniquely bring. No one can take God's gifts and purposes out of our hands. Don't sacrifice those gifts by picking up lies hurled at you in the dark.

We lay down the promises of God when we:

- Believe we are unworthy of goodness or love, continuing to live small, powerless lives.
- Believe the accusations drawn against us, turning to wield the same lies against others.
- Allow our hearts to become hardened by the pain we have gone through, putting up walls of self-protection.

Partnering with these lies is an agreement with destruction, with anti-love. There are people who are struggling, who want to give up, who are waiting for you to fight for what is true. People who need you to bring the gifts you carry, and the lessons you've learned, with courage and wholeness. You have always carried great gifts. The battles you have faced can forge a great weapon to set others free.

Redeeming Our Reality

When life is ugly, God is ready to get in the dirt with us and begin creating unthinkable displays of beauty. God is the Redeemer.

I love tearing words apart. One day, I couldn't get this word *redeem* out of my head. It was November 2020, and Duncan and I were meeting with our counselor once again via Zoom. This time, he wanted to meet with each of us individually to discuss permanently separating. We had been trying to repair our marriage for about eight months and had come to a roadblock. I didn't want our marriage to end, yet we didn't know how to move forward together.

While Duncan was talking to the counselor, I went for a walk and prayed. *God, there is nothing you can't redeem*, I declared. That last word stood out to me. I said it over and over:

RE-deem.

re-DEEM.

DEEM... What is that?

I know what "RE" is. I know what a *REdo* is, a *REmodel*, and even *REcognize* makes sense. But *REdeem*? An again-deem? What does that mean? Does your brain do this to you?

I stopped in my tracks and pulled out my phone to look up *deem*. Mirriam-Webster defines *deem* as "to come to think or judge: consider."[1] Deem is the verdict, the final say, on a situation or person. It's what we have decided a situation is, or is not. We often *deem* a person worthy or unworthy, forgivable or unforgivable. Or we *deem* a situation reparable or irreparable. Taking in all of the facts and judging accordingly with our words and actions, we determine the final verdict.

To *deem* a situation is to give it a name. What we name or call a situation will become a reality.

It looked as though my story and marriage were *irreparable*. I was *rejected and a failure*. Our family was now *broken*. These were the facts, according to what I could see. I wonder how often we decide something is impossible and beyond repair that God longs to RE-deem.

> *I wonder how often we decide something is impossible and beyond repair that God longs to RE-deem.*

The reality we face may be of divorce, death, sickness, or moral or financial failure. Is God declaring life, loyalty, blessing, and connection in spite of these facts?

During that walk, I declared, without much positive emotion flowing, that this marriage was *not beyond repair*. I prayed that instead of *irreparable*, God would declare the final verdict of our marriage as *better than ever, whole and beautiful*. Where betrayal had cut and caused division, I declared that *love and faithfulness will never leave this house*.

There were times when I would pray and declare these things, while still not being sure our marriage would make it. My prayers for "what could be" were that *my husband will be a godly man of integrity and faithfulness*. I honestly didn't always have hope that it would be Duncan. But I knew that God is good and faithful, even when others make choices that you wish they wouldn't. Don't get me wrong—I also prayed for Duncan. But there were times I prayed into what could be, without attaching my hope to his free will. Duncan could make the choice to walk away. I needed to have my hope anchored to Jesus and His ability to redeem *anything*, not in what another person may or may not choose.

Calling Things as God Sees Them

Each day, we are agreeing with either a truth or a lie. Are our agreements what God has declared to be true, or are they what circumstances are screaming to be called? It's time to call things as God sees them. Listen to God's heart as He aches to redeem your situation, and then speak out the redeemed reality He reveals.

One way I have learned to distinguish between my thoughts and God's voice deep within my heart is to follow the clues that love leaves. I am not naturally hope-filled, forgiving, gracious, or life-giving. But God is. In difficult situations, when my shadows come to the surface, I have learned to be still and listen for the Voice of Love. Love will bring hope and forgiveness. Love will desire another's best.

God spoke into my heart that *betrayal* was not to become my identity. I wrote in my journal as I felt God speak to me,

> *Don't let this become your identity. It feels as if your pain won't be validated if you don't hold onto it. Your pain is valid. It is real. Let it go. Release your right for justice, revenge, or even feeling validated or understood. Release those needs and desires to Me. Watch as I release into you My life, peace, and hope. There is purpose beyond this pain, beauty from ashes. I can bring all of the frayed hopes, shattered dreams, crumbling emotions together into the most beautiful outcome. Betrayal is not your story. Don't let it become your identity. Don't let pain become your identity.*

The day Duncan and I decided we could no longer be married was a pivotal moment for my heart. I was able to release my need for circumstances to turn out the way I wanted. I began to trust that whatever happened to me, or our marriage, God would make it good. This opened the door for God to RE-name what was, and to help me declare what could be.

A Prayer of Redemption

Declaring God's Word and praying are often intertwined activities for me. If such an approach feels new and awkward to you, or if you cannot muster your own words amidst the pain, I offer the following prayer from my journal as a starting place for your conversation with God. When we look to Jesus and hold onto His promises, we may not see the situation change. But how we see the circumstance will absolutely change. Whisper this prayer, shout it, or meditate on it, remembering that God has *RE-deemed* you, and that in His sight, nothing in this life is irreparable:

God, you alone bring life from death, beauty from ashes. You call what is not into being. You know the end of this story and call it good. You redeem the past, and you carve out a way through the storm for me. You are strength in my weakness. A light of hope in the dark, drawing me out.

Nothing is wasted, and all will be set right one day. Today, I entrust all of it to you. Thank you, Jesus. You are good and do only good.

- EIGHT -
Dusty Trails and Messy Rivers

I came to a place in overcoming pain where it wasn't enough that my marriage could be made whole. I wanted a multiplication back of what was lost. I wanted back what was stolen from Duncan, the girls, and me in this season of undoing.

A biblical proverb states that if a man is caught stealing, *he must pay back seven times what he stole.*[1] The devil, through lies and deceit, had stolen from us, and I decided that I wanted my multiplied return. I began to pray for a multiplication of all that was lost and stolen—for my heart, for our children, for our marriage, for our finances, everything! *Multiply it ALL, God!* I prayed. I began declaring *ten times what was lost*. I'm not sure why I chose ten. The proverb clearly says seven. Maybe I'm an overachiever.

A Penny Now, a Dime Later

A friend from college used to say, "A penny now, or a dime later." The meaning being, you could settle for a penny today, or through intentionality and patience, whether building a relationship or a business, have ten times more in the future. I decided that it was time to stop settling for pennies and start collecting my dimes. I find it interesting that biblically and mathematically, the number 10 represents completeness and wholeness. That was what my heart was really asking for: wholeness in every area.

I spend a lot of time during our Colorado summers mountain biking. We have an incredible trail system not far from us that consists of miles and miles of dirt roads and single track (trails just wide enough for bikes). An average bike ride begins with the dirt roads from the trailhead parking lot to the start of whatever trail I'm riding that day . . . connecting single-track trails together to make a loop back to the parking lot.

A handful of camping spots line the dirt roads in this high-desert, sage country. There is no pavement. No coffee shop. No park ranger station or tourist attractions. Unless trails and rocks and sage are your thing. And on a bike, they are totally my thing.

One particular day in the summer of 2020, I was flooded with negative thoughts and emotions. Wanting to avoid people, I drove out to the trailhead where fewer people go. I was about three miles up a lonely dirt road when it first happened. I was praying, complaining, hurting, and trying to remember the lessons about redemption, hope, and love that God had been walking me through. The sun was bouncing off something lodged in the dirt so brightly that I had to stop and see what it was.

It was a dime stuck, but not buried, in the middle of this nowhere road. It would have been easy to miss if the sun hadn't hit it just right. I pried it out of the packed dirt road with my fingernail and put it in my pack. And I wondered, my heart full at this message and confirmation of my prayers. Not a penny. Not a quarter. A dime. Ten. *God, multiply back ten times what was lost.* I laughed at this tangible and insignificant disk of metal that held so much significance. A token that God was present and faithful, and that His promise of wholeness was available for me today.

I now have about twenty dimes stashed in my desk drawer. Found in unexpected places, lonely back-of-the-map trails, sidewalks, and parks. A glimmer catches my eye, another dime for my collection, to remind me that God not only redeems; He multiplies and brings wholeness. He continually reminded me that He had heard my prayers and was at work to make them a reality. His heart's cry was also for wholeness in my life.

It's His desire for you, also. Dare to ask God for a multiplication of what was stolen from you, and watch expectantly for His tokens of love to drop into your everyday life. They probably won't be the same as mine, maybe not dimes, but they'll be something that speaks directly from His heart to yours.

I am amazed that something so simple as a dime in the dirt could hold so much meaning. Tokens of God's goodness, reminders that He is faithful to hear and answer our prayers. He is faithful to restore more than what was lost, and to redeem every story. We don't need to settle for anything less.

A Broken Heart's Whisper

An unexpected gift was given when my heart was broken open. Jesus met me in ways that were so intimate, so beautiful, ways that could only be found in the raw moments of desperation. I found Jesus to be true to His Word as He poured healing life into my wounded soul. He drew near to my broken heart, just as He promises in the Bible. One day, I wrote this in my journal:

What if
In pain, we find wholeness,
And tears that bring healing.
In the breaking, there is becoming,
Sadness gives way to joy.
In the test, you find your strength.

God isn't interested in our achievements or acts of devotion. What He longs for is our heart—our inmost and most intimate being. Broken hearts release rare and beautiful worship, as every drop of pain, hope, fear, and love is poured out. This is the fragrance of surrender. When everything is lost, we remind ourselves that Jesus was all we had to begin with.

> *Broken hearts release rare and beautiful worship, as every drop of pain, hope, fear, and love is poured out. This is the fragrance of surrender.*

I am supposed to say it was my faith-filled worship that began to shift the reality of our marriage. In reality, it was the whisper of a broken heart: *Jesus, help.* When words failed me and grief flooded my thoughts, He was near.

Emotional Debris

Colorado springtime is marked by rivers that swell and surge as the high mountain snowpack melts. Although the rivers are clear and peaceful the rest of the year, the spring melt causes these waters to tumble and roll at capacity. Sticks and debris left along the riverbank by winter's shedding are swept up in the muddy flood.

Healing is messy and debris filled too. Don't be discouraged; you won't always be a mess. As muddy feelings swirl and cloud, long-entrenched lies break free. Like sticks and leaves in a river, our wounds and disappointments are caught up in the flood and swept away.

I wish the broken world hadn't landed on my doorstep. Yet I couldn't deny the presence of Jesus with me through every step through the shattered pieces. At times, I could feel myself slipping into hardness, and mistrust of everyone around me. I would think I was healing up nicely, when a song, a thought, or a certain smell would send me reeling into fear, hatred, and shame all over again. The rocks were loosening. The debris was getting washed up. It was beautiful and ugly, grace filled, and hard. Love was flowing again. And it was messy.

I found my way back to love and trust by facing the pain. I have seen too many people end up hardened, bitter, and broken for far too long. It felt impossible at times to pray or worship. These acts highlight the hatred, anger, and fear inside me. *Ugh. Will I always be broken?* I wondered. *Is there anything good beyond this point?* Grace flowed powerfully, but this, too, felt painful at times, and all I could do was weep as love washed me clean.

Topping it all off, I didn't sleep well. Thoughts and images assaulted my imagination. Fear closing in to devour my mind and body. For a long time, I could only sleep with earbuds in. I would play the Psalms from the Bible, or soft worship music. Sometimes I would just leave the earbuds in with nothing playing. This helped block out the sounds of the world going on as if nothing had happened. With the sounds around muted, the questions and accusations were also silenced. I would finally fall asleep, only to wake in the morning crying as my first conscious memory was of betrayal.

Healing is hard. It is easier to numb ourselves through work, substances, food, endless processing with others, or exercise that pushes us to complete exhaustion. We are at risk of erecting strict adherence to our discipline of choice—an illusion that keeps us feeling safe and in control, be it religious, spiritual, physical, or any other list of personal dogmas we can control. Beliefs that once served us have turned into rules that make us feel safe, but constrain us.

The temptation is to create a comfortable world in which we don't need Jesus in our day-to-day lives. Staying "safe" along the riverbank, distracted from the wounds festering inside. Love is flowing in the mess, waiting for us to dive in and find peace and healing. But I wonder (and we'll look at this question next), *Do we really want to be made well?*

- NINE -
The Reasons We Stay Broken

Jesus asks an interesting question in John 5:6 (NKJV): "Do you want to be made well?" He asks it of a man who had been sick for thirty-eight years. In the Amplified Bible translation,[1] John 5:5 reads,

> There was a certain man there who had suffered with a deep-seated and lingering disorder for thirty-eight years.

Deep-seated. Disorder. Thirty. Eight. Years.

This man had a list thirty-eight years long of reasons he *could not* be well. Reasons why *this is just the way things are*, and a history of failed attempts. We all do. But the question is not, *What's between you and your healing?* Jesus is not concerned in this moment with any demonic force, physical deformity, or mental ailment that blocks our path to freedom.

The question Jesus asks is, "Do you *want* to become well?" Look at John 5:6 in the Amplified translation:

> When Jesus noticed him lying there [helpless], knowing that he had already been a long time in that condition, He said to him, Do

you want to become well? [Are you really in earnest about getting well?]

Similar to our own reasons for not being able to be well, the man explains that there is no one to help him. If we let them, our excuses become validation for how hard our life is, and why it's okay for us to remain broken. Worse, others push ahead of this man every time he tries to reach the healing waters:

> The invalid answered, Sir, I have nobody when the water is moving to put me into the pool; but while I am trying to come [into it] myself, somebody else steps down ahead of me. John 5:7 AMPC

Neglect! Injustice! Abuse!

Jesus doesn't ask us if we are *able* to find our way to wholeness. He doesn't ask us *how* those around us are finding their way to healing. He doesn't ask about *the obstacles* in our way to healing. He asks just one question: Do we *want to be whole?*

I don't know if we really do. We like the idea of being whole, but not the process or the responsibility. Becoming whole can be painfully scary, and embarrassingly messy. We will no longer be able to sit on our mats of excuses, ruminating on the injustices of our past. Our broken theology will have to be thrown out the window as God declares, *I have always wanted you to be whole, but do you want it?*

The story continues:

> Jesus said to him, Get up! Pick up your bed (sleeping pad) and walk! Instantly the man became well and recovered his strength and picked up his bed and walked. But that happened on the Sabbath. John 5:8–9 AMPC

Can you imagine?! Commanding someone so sick that he could barely move to *get up, get over it, and walk out of here* . . . Here is what's fascinating: The man never answers the question. I love that Jesus knows our desires, even the ones barely a whisper within our hearts. I believe Jesus saw the man's desire to be well, and his faith to obey the craziest of instructions. And that is what's needed to counter the gravitational pull of the mats we have become so accustomed to.

This man had a choice. He could look at the excuses he was lying on and pick them up. He could step into a brand-new life. Or he could choose to stay where he was, with what he knew to be familiar and safe. Sure, he was thirty-eight years into a deep-seated disorder, but he knew that life. There were no surprises. Though painful and restricting, many people choose to stay physically, emotionally, or mentally bedridden, even as Jesus proclaims with power and promise, *Pick up your mat and walk!*

Being made well often requires a change in location, relationships, and mindsets. We cannot stay on the mats of broken dreams, toxic relationships, betrayal, or trauma. Remaining in the company of those who glory in their infirmities and disorders, replaying the same powerless soundtracks on repeat, is no longer an option.

Pinned to the Mat

Do we like the mat that keeps us bound, because it declares to all the world how unfair our life has been? Does the mat we lie on somehow validate the difficulty of our situation? It's hard to believe we could really be free, and the journey isn't lined with cheerleaders. There are no witnesses to the deep healing of the heart. This is an inside job few will be able to see, and even fewer understand. It's easier to stop and set up our mat as a monument to the pain of the past for all to see, so people will validate our pain, or at least be forced to acknowledge all we've been through.

Do you want to be made well, or is the attention you gain from being broken your reward?

I could still be lying on a mat of betrayal, making sure everyone around me knew the how, why, when, and where behind my brokenness. Instead, I trusted that if Jesus said I could get up and walk, I could get up and walk. There were days this felt ridiculous, and impossible. How could such a deep wound ever stop hurting? Some days felt as if I would be broken forever. I crawled and stumbled, getting up once again, with knees and hands bruised as I learned to pick up my mat of shame, humiliation, and fear to take a few more steps forward.

It isn't ridiculous or impossible to be truly whole. Not only can we walk again—we can run! To be whole, we need to have this conversation with Jesus and be real about our answer. When He says *get up and walk*, will we respond with action? Or will we remind Him of all of the unfair, unjust, and impossible reasons that we cannot simply *get up, pick up our mat, and be free*?

Except we can. If Jesus says we can, then staying bound and broken is entirely our choice.

Jesus knows what we need. He may address the unforgiveness we are dragging around. Or maybe address the religious spirit that needs to be left behind. It might be time to address any addictions and distractions. In His presence, everything keeping us pinned to the mat can be undone. Our fearful, wounded hearts will kick and scream, doing anything to avoid real exposure.

Kick, scream, cry, and whatever you do, find your way to God's love.

Why we are broken might be someone else's fault. But why we are still broken is entirely our own choice. Cracking our hearts open and allowing love to flow into the rocky places means we are no longer protected by the walls of distractions, addictions, busyness, rage, fear, or self-pity.

> *Why we are broken might be someone else's fault. But why we are still broken is entirely our own choice.*

Walls of self-protection, built with the stones of our pain, will prevent us from entering into an intimate encounter with God. God wants to tear down these walls so His love can heal the pain threatening to sear and callous our hearts. Just in case you think you're too far gone, your issues too deep, and your habits too entrenched to be free, Jesus seeks out *this* man for that very reason. It is time to get well.

Not a One-and-Done Process

Please hear my heart: I am not suggesting that Jesus is saying, *Get over it and get out of here with your issues*. When Jesus says it's time to move on, He gives us the power to no longer be bound by past wounds, bitterness, anger, resentment, and fear. We all come to a point in healing when more talking only reopens the wounds.

When Jesus meets us in our pain, His words and presence are the strategies and power we need to be free. The problem is, in His presence we have to face our inability, brokenness, and pain.

I wish I could tell you this is a one-and-done process. It's not. The discussion with our counselor in November 2020 did not end in separation or divorce. My heart had released the outcome, as I allowed Duncan to make his choice. If he wanted to leave, I wasn't going to stop him. And somehow, everything shifted in that moment. Duncan chose to rebuild trust, take the steps to repair our marriage, and meet me in the pain for as long as it took for me to heal.

Still, I had many days when all of the pain and fear came full strength to the surface, one, two, even three years later. It's like getting caught in an eddy on a river. I would be flowing downstream nicely, enjoying life, when I would look up and suddenly realize I was swirling endlessly, surrounded by the debris I had thought was long gone.

When triggers sneak up on me, I can remind my heart of the promises God has given me. I intentionally focus my attention on His love. As I do this, I find myself exiting the swirling emotions and getting back into the river of love and peace.

Learning to pause and listen was one way I found to *pick up my mat*. When I felt anxious and afraid, I would stop what I was doing, put my hand on my heart, and pause. Breathe. And say, out loud, "You are okay. You are safe. Your marriage is healing." I wasn't lying; all those statements were true. I needed my body and emotions to remember it. I needed my ears to hear this declaration.

I'm learning to navigate the river more adeptly. I can look up and see the eddies, and avoid getting sucked into them. I have learned to pray specifically over my thoughts, and even my physical neurological pathways. I have learned to watch for spiritual agreements that want to flip my little raft in the rapids. (I talk more about such unhealthy, unholy agreements, and the strategies for finding freedom from them, in chapter 21, *"ROAD CLOSED."*)

Jesus is good and kind. He will not hurt us. He wants us to be free. The walls we build, and the agreements we've made to protect our hearts, are hurting us and keeping us stuck on the mat.

He has so much more for us than a life stuck on the mat. If that's the life we choose, however, He will let us remain there, and will still love us. He will never force us off the mat. We must *want* to exchange all of its security and comfort for wholeness.

Our healing isn't going to come from going to church or doing good Christian things. It isn't found in the next great self-help book. Counseling has a part to play, but nothing can do what Jesus can. It's easy to go to church and call it good. It seems comforting in the moment to talk about issues and acquiesce to head-knowledge "healing" over heart-tenderizing wholeness.

Some people display their broken trust in God through fully embracing all sorts of sinful acts. Others who have long abandoned trust in Him find their comfort in continuing in the safety of Christian disciplines and community. Church, counseling, books, podcasts, talking things out with friends . . . these things are not bad and can help you heal. But it is Jesus who sets the captives free.

We want to know that fighting for love and doing it well matters. That our prayers and tears and learning and growing and healing will make a difference for our family, for our hearts, and maybe for others. As we rest, fight, struggle, and find Jesus, we begin envisioning a life beyond this pain. Envisioning how God can weave and craft and turn a horrible circumstance into a beautiful path for ourselves, and for helping others become free too. This is hope.

PART TWO

becoming unstuck

to no longer be stuck.[1]

to be released from being glued, fastened, or bound.[2]

- TEN -
The Reality of Being Stuck

As a follower of Jesus, I am not exempt from missing out on the life He offers. I could feel myself suffocating as I attempted to protect my heart. Living in hell while waiting for heaven's rescue. The consequence of self-protection is that we create a downsized life. A scared heart builds walls. The walls we build look like busy activity and good stewardship. Their real names are isolation and distraction. Yet it is possible to step past the pain of yesterday into a life of intimacy, fun, and freedom.

I led a youth group at a small church for about ten years. For most of the kids, it was something to do on an otherwise boring Monday night. And there were snacks. One night still stands out to me. We were in the living-room area of the church, talking about God and eternity. I must have asked the kids if they believed in heaven and hell. Sarah, a rough-and-tough teen, moved slowly in a hand-me-down rocking chair before speaking up. I'll never forget what she said: "I think hell is doing something that I love, like playing hockey, forever, but never being able to enjoy it."

Mic. Drop.

To this day, that's the best description of life without God I have ever heard.

Not from a pulpit or a renowned Christian evangelist. But from a kid struggling to figure out what Jesus and heaven and hell and life and death are all about. I see so many people living beautiful, successful lives, enjoying none of it.

If we're not careful, our internal struggles with unforgiveness, bitterness, and fear will keep us chained to the past. Even as I healed and learned to rewrite my story, I often felt stuck.

I felt as if something was broken inside as I struggled to enjoy fun and happy moments, and connect with the smiles and laughter of my girls or friends. As our marriage healed and was becoming healthier than ever, I still struggled to be in the new reality before me.

I was living a good life, while continually being pulled into the past. I felt defeated and afraid. Surrounded by the best, enjoying none of it. Living in an emotional and mental hell. How often have we arrived in a new day and a bright future, only to rewrite yesterday's failures on the clean, white pages of this new day?

Have you ever spoken with people who still talk about being mistreated or wounded decades ago? The way they tell the story sounds as though it happened only yesterday. They are stuck. I had to recognize and deal with the thoughts and memories that felt so real, telling me that I was still in danger, still being mistreated, and that I still wasn't safe. The fear of being hurt again was real. The fear of becoming someone who never finds her way out of pain kept me working through every knotted emotion to unravel the mess within my soul. And I knew that I could not break free by reliving the past every day.

We can't create a new and beautiful future by watching yesterday's reruns. This is my friend Sarah's description of hell. Living every day with the promises of life, peace, and joy before us, unable to take hold of any of it.

The pain that we don't address will begin to feel so normal that we lose any context for what life is without it. This is what keeps many bound to the past, and stuck in pain.

Avoiding and Coping

Our souls will suffocate when we try to protect our future from the past. Where is the key to this prison door?

I have never been a good liar. I'm actually an oversharer. Avoiding what hurt wasn't going to work for me. It doesn't work for anyone, but some people are just better at lying to themselves. Avoidance is not the way to freedom. Attempting to cover up pain or look for ways to meet legitimate needs in illegitimate ways is like slapping a Band-Aid on wounds that need a surgeon.

No one likes seeing those they love in pain. So often, I was told by people close to me that it was time to just get over what happened. Yet no one could map out good steps for doing that. If I could have shed the broken heart and ditched the flashbacks, I would have, in a heartbeat. So I pretended I was okay. I showed up, served, and did what the people around me needed me to do, so *they* would be okay. My healing might have come faster if I had trusted my heart. Avoidance and denial are not great ways to heal.

It felt like running endlessly on a hamster wheel. I was exhausted. There is tension in healing. To heal wholly, we must grieve wholly. Running from what is broken takes us right back to where we started. The circumstances might look different each time, but the issues that need to be addressed will be the same.

> *Our only option is to go through all of the mess and pain with God, into a new and beautiful future.*

A common response to pain is looking to coping mechanisms. We want to slow down our racing heart, end the swirling negative thoughts, or numb the pain of our broken soul. Band-Aids of addiction cannot soothe the self-hatred raging within you. Another relationship cannot meet the needs in your heart that you won't address. Running to the next Christian conference won't heal what you refuse to confess. One more business deal can't make you feel worthy. Jesus alone can reveal and heal what is holding us back from freedom. Our only option is to go through all of the mess and pain with God, into a new and beautiful future.

Jesus in the Ashes

I employed a common, yet powerful Christian practice as I healed and battled for our marriage: Communion. Communion reminds me of who Jesus is, and all He has given to those who will follow Him.

When I look at Jesus, I find hope. At His feet, I remember that nothing is beyond repair, and nothing is impossible. Duncan and I could have a good marriage. Our family could be whole. In these moments, my focus was on a future full of promise. I trusted that my future was good because Jesus was there. He alone was able to turn these ashes into beauty.

Communion is a powerful gift. It is an act in which we receive the life, protection, and healing of Jesus. This practice does not require a priest or worship team. You can commune with God from your home, or your car during your lunch break. For a while, I had a box of Communion elements from Amazon; the Styrofoam-flavored wafer, and dark purple liquid with a questionable expiration date. When that supply ran out, I would grab a pinch of bread and a sip of kombucha from the fridge. It was important for me to keep this simple and not overthink it. Rather than worrying about having the right juice (or wine) or handmade artisan bread, I did my best to keep the heart of the process as my focus—connecting with Jesus and receiving His life.

Closing my eyes, I envision Jesus on the cross. I approach Him with the broken memories, thoughts, emotions, and betrayals of all kinds. I imagine myself setting all of it in a pile at His feet. All of the anger, the pain, the fear. He has become all of the ugly and wrong in me and in the world, and He has conquered it once and for all. Even if I could carry these burdens, they would hinder me from moving into a new and whole future.

I hold the bread reverently in my hands. "This is My body," Jesus says, and in eating it we have life, as He has it. So I take all the things that are not full of life and lay them at the foot of the cross. Still holding the bread, I begin to thank Jesus for His body. He was broken so I could be made whole. He carried my sin and shame to the grave, so I could be delivered. He waged a war on darkness, so I could be victorious. This crumb in my hand represents an exchange—my life for His, His life for mine. I eat and remember, and am thankful.

Next, I hold the cup, again with reverence and awe, believing that the act of receiving it brings life. Jesus said, "This is the new covenant . . . poured out as a sacrifice for you." I remember the original communion meal in the time of Moses, a lamb's blood on the doorpost of each home, which turned away death and destruction. I declare the power of Jesus' blood over my marriage, my children, my husband, our finances, our health, our everything. I remember Abraham's covenant with God—an exchange of lives, God's for ours, ours for God's. His victories are ours. His hope is ours. His life is ours. His goodness is ours. His peace is ours. I declare the power of the blood Jesus carried and released so that we could receive and be free.

Communion is much more than a religious discipline. It is a powerful declaration and reminder of the power of Jesus becoming sin, and releasing His life to all who would receive it. We can take Communion in our own homes, at any time of the day. It is a powerful and life-giving meal that we are invited to receive.

This was one way I was able to release all the darkness and pain within me. I do realize that there are some memories too painful to revisit without the help of a therapist or someone trained in trauma. You may need help bringing the wounds into the open for healing, and that's okay. Yet also do whatever you can to help yourself—like spending time at the Communion table, at the foot of the cross, where you can lay it all down. Do whatever is needed to be whole. The world is waiting for you to rise up and write the rest of your story.

- ELEVEN -
How Stories Are Written

In fourth grade, my class received a brand-new Apple computer. Our teacher, Ms. Hovis, assigned our class a project on that hulk of 1990 technology. We were each given five minutes to write part of a story, adding to what the person before us had written. When our turn was over, another student would step up to the keyboard to continue. At the end of everyone's turn, Ms. Hovis read the story aloud to the class.

I sat down to write. Using my classmates' words as a launching pad, I knew exactly how to make this a great story! The time ended too quickly as I entrusted the vision to my fellow fourth graders. Surely, they would see the brilliance of the path I was going down and continue to take the story in that direction.

No. Not even close. I remember listening, horrified, as the story twisted and turned into silly, spooky, and downright crazy directions. Not at all where it *should* have gone. Had the others even read what I wrote?! The other kids seemed to have written whatever, willy-nilly, came to mind. While the rest of the class giggled and cheered at how the group project had turned out, my ten-year-old heart sank with disappointment. I had taken the assignment seriously, attempting to create something profound. I was excited to use the computer and to write! The problem was that it wasn't my story alone to craft. The vision in my heart wasn't the only one being written.

It dawns on me that this is often how we experience life. Excited and ready, a word from God in our heart, pen in hand, we are ready to create a beautiful story. Reality crashes in as others, who have access to their own pens, begin writing alongside and even on top of our stories. Some will choose to craft evil choices, unforgiveness, shame, and fear. They seem unaware that this is not how our story was supposed to unfold. The actions of others twist and wind into our story, until what we thought would be is no longer recognizable.

As the souls of broken people bled onto my carefully crafted pages, God was with me. The words God pens are good, not evil. Hope and beauty flow from His heart, writing over fear with love. Illuminating the dark corners with beauty and light. Sketching images of what our future could be. But could I trust Him to bring life to the evil in front of me?

God loves to create beautiful stories, but will never overrule the story that we choose. I was battling to overcome the story I found myself in. Themes of *betrayed, divorced,* and *rejected* threatened to permanently define my life. Would I partner with these outcomes, or with what God said could be?

From a window overlooking the beauty and strength of the unmoving mountain range to the north, I often wrote and declared what God whispered to my heart. *What is true is that I am loved by God. Chosen, and not rejected, no matter how another human responds to me.* I declared that the legacy of my house would be love and faithfulness, strength, emotional health, and relational wisdom. Promises I found written in my Bible were held as real and as unmoving as the mountain peaks I was gazing at. Weapons forged against my future, and my family's legacy, would not have the final say. God's words of hope guided my story back to power, love ,and a sound mind. Jesus is both the source of our story of faith and the one who will guide us to the ending.

God was writing into my heart vision, strength, and beauty for a future that seemed impossible. Some days, it took all of my strength to declare it out loud. I knew that I needed to hear my voice proclaiming His words so hope could take root in my soul.

My instinct in the face of the worst of what people could be and do was to withdraw from them all access to the pages of my story. If no one is allowed to write on these pages, then I am in control. I am safe. In a deeper, quieter place, I knew that retreating wouldn't erase all risk of more harm. But shutting everyone out would mean closing the door to love and joy. People with good intentions, though imperfect, could no longer write goodness and strength into my story.

Great stories are written in community. Hopelessness grows in isolation. Community requires humility and vulnerability. We need each other to bring out our best stories, especially when evil has declared *The End*. Isolation is so tempting: *I don't need anyone. I can do this on my own!* Then there's the most arrogant statement humanity has made: *I don't need God*. We may claim that we would never shut God out, but when we shut people out, we close the door to His influence and love through them.

A biblical proverb says, *If you build a wall, you attract a thief*.[1] Hearts shutting out the world invite confusion and torment as the walls close in. Self-protection promises safety, but delivers destruction. Building towers of isolation invites the destroyer. Who else would know we're in trouble? Who would see the pages now scribbled over with lies of shame and fear? No one, for the walls are high, and the gates have locked out the community that could help us cross out *The End* and replace it with *Part Two*.

As I write these words, I am aware that I haven't written with the same child-like boldness since that day in fourth grade. The disappointment of losing a part of what I desired to create marked me. The shame, humiliation, and fear brought on by the painful actions of others now threaten to take away our boldness and courage to create the future we desire most. Our future requires that we invite others to write alongside us, and even on top of our story, as we trust God to make it all beautiful in the end.

Finding God in the Story

You and I are eternal beings, dwelling both outside of time and inside of it. We are both spiritual and physical beings. God is not restricted by place or time. He is at the beginning of our story and the end. He sees every desire and decision. He knows every impact brokenness has had on our hearts. He has gone ahead of us, carving out new paths to the finish line. He goes behind us, bringing closure to the good and bad chapters that tempt us to remain in what is finished. He is awaiting our next step, our next choice. And He knows what we will choose, because He has been in our future and has made the way good.

One of my favorite lines from the Bible is Jeremiah 29:11: "'For I know the plans I have for you,' says the Lord. 'They are plans for good and not for disaster, to give you a future and a hope.'"

What I have found as I've grown in my understanding of God's nature is that His plans are not a set path that we can mess up or miss. Instead, this verse conveys how God dreamed of and created us with specific intention, ingenuity, beauty, and design to be a dwelling place for His Spirit. God's imagination is unlimited! He starts our story with so much curiosity, imagination, and intention, and anticipates how we will live this life, using the personality and talents He has woven into our being.

> ***Here's the truth: We cannot miss God if we are seeking Him, and He has not lost sight of us.***

How often have I approached God with the view that His plans are limited to one idea, one route, and one set of very intricate, specific steps for me to take to get to the *good future and hope* promised? That if I mess up, I miss everything, even God. Here's the truth: We cannot miss God if we are seeking Him, and He has not lost sight of us. His plan is that we would become the curious, beautiful, creative dwelling places for His presence that He imagined we could be.

Life is not easy, but it can be good. I found myself in a story that I never imagined. I had to believe that this was not the end. God says His plans are good, and the situation I found myself in was far from good. Knowing He was already in my future gave me hope that the story would become beautiful.

Waiting on God

I find it interesting that Jesus seems more concerned with our *unbelief* than our *sins*. Belief is trusting that God is good and does only good. Trusting that He will do what He says He will do. Trusting that He is who He says He is. Trust is not just a creed. It is action and movement. If I say I believe God is good, then I must do something with that. I must wake up ready to build, create, and grow. I enter my day seeking to be filled with love and the grace to impact others with this goodness. Trusting that God is good keeps us safe from the allure of choosing things that promise relief from suffering, but bring destruction.

Unbelief is the disease; sin is the symptom.

Attempting to write a beautiful story comes with risk. I could be disappointed and hurt when life does not unfold as hoped. Setbacks and failures that seem insurmountable could provide opportunities to quit. I could conclude that God never wanted me to be a co-creator in my story. I could believe that no matter how or what I contribute, I cannot change my future. I know many who have surrendered their pen to these lies.

Instead, I chose to believe that God does want me to build, create, and grow. Some people with the "life will be what it will be" mentality wrongly call their inaction *waiting on God*. Sitting idly by, hoping, even praying, that a thriving business, healthy family, or great relationships will manifest.

I've never made progress by waiting for God to do *my part*.

The idea of *waiting on God* is a grossly misused and misinterpreted reality for many followers of Jesus. The beautiful promise of a good future and hope has been whittled down by some who are too afraid to believe that their story can be so much more than what they have known. Others would rather remain in their small but comfortable life, foregoing the adventures that would stretch and grow their heart and faith.

Often, our view of God's goodness isn't tarnished by what God has or has not done. Our perception is damaged by what *others* have or have not done. When it becomes painful to love and be loved, we want to shut the doors and close the blinds. Yes, times of quiet and meditation are powerful and necessary when coupled with real relationships. But chronic isolation from healthy community is dangerous. We end up floating around in a monastic-like attitude of waiting on God, sounding super-spiritual, while we are actually avoiding God and people at all costs.

Love becomes a heart posture when put to the test in real life relationships. Until then, it's only a nice-sounding principle. We cannot learn to love outside of community. We cannot receive the fullness of God's goodness and love in isolation.

If you are waiting on God in this season, can I ask you, Are you waiting, ready to act on your next step into the future God desires for you? Or are you waiting to be rescued from the hard parts of your story?

Waiting for rescue creates an atmosphere that normalizes inaction and unbelief. I could interpret my situation—a lack of divine rescue—to mean that it's just not God's time, when the reality is that my habits and unbelief are keeping me from taking a step into the future. I could make excuses like *God knows my heart,* as my pain runs over the people He has given me to love.

Yet I have decided that I will no longer excuse, spiritualize, or normalize being stuck. When I find myself approaching a problem with this kind of powerlessness, I must choose to shift my perspective and take action. This means that I choose to be honest about why I'm not growing or moving forward. I choose to apologize, stay humble, and admit a mistake. I choose to allow truth to uncover the lies, habits, and fears that are keeping me from acting on what I say I believe.

God is limitless and has designed each one of us to create without limit. The only thing that will stop us from authoring a beautiful life is remaining stuck in our broken past, broken mindset, or broken trust. Instead, we can begin each day with an invitation to God to scribe His desires on our hearts, while we, pen in hand, live to make the dream a reality. It's time to show up bravely, turn the page, and begin to write again.

Annie's Marriage Is . . .

I struggled daily for nearly two years to keep my thoughts and beliefs aligned with hope for a good future. Shortly after the Zoom call with our counselor to discuss separation, I found a prerecorded "Save Your Marriage" workshop for about $200 advertised on Facebook. It was a last-ditch effort, but I bought it. The course wasn't about changing my spouse, or manipulation tactics to get my marriage partner to finally see things my way. It was 99% focused on changing *my heart and mindsets.*

One of the very first workshop exercises was to write out a vision statement in the third person. It was both freeing and difficult to dream and imagine a good future, while living in so much pain. I didn't realize until much later how powerful and necessary an exercise like this is. Here's an excerpt from what I wrote:

> *Annie's marriage is full of fun and adventure, love and loyalty. She and Duncan love building businesses and ministries, and dreaming together. Annie's marriage is emotionally, physically, and spiritually safe, connected, loving, and fulfilling. Annie feels safe knowing that Duncan is committed to the marriage, and he has set boundaries in place to protect her heart, and their relationship. They have both put in the work to change and overcome obstacles, in order to build real connection and understanding in their relationship.*
>
> *The deep love they feel for each other and from each other is more than either of them ever hoped for. Outsiders often wonder how they rebuilt such a beautiful, powerful, flirty, fun, committed relationship after going through such a difficult season. Because of what they have overcome, and have built, they daily are a source of hope and inspiration to many people.*

It felt ridiculous to write this. It couldn't have been further from our reality. I would read it out loud, so my heart could hope for more than what I was seeing. Some days, I wasn't sure that Duncan would be this person, so I exchanged his name for *Annie's husband*. No matter the outcome of this situation, I had a part to play in what I believed and declared about my future.

I am amazed looking back and reading these words almost five years later. So much of what I wrote down has come true. If we dare to dream and invite others into our story, nothing is impossible.

I'm Stuck! Now What?

Practically, the process toward wholeness requires forgiveness, boundaries, and praying for those who have hurt us. In praying for others, we will see them as God does and will be able to declare God's desires over them. Praying for those who have wounded us deeply causes us to see from God's perspective and position of love.

Through gritted teeth and a pounding heart, I prayed life, restoration, and blessing over those who had wounded me so deeply. Those who had betrayed, those who had gossiped, those who had told me to just move on, and those who were also collateral damage in this mess . . . I prayed, I blessed, I chose love.

Often, however, as soon as the words were out of my mouth I would jump to accusations, anger, and fear. Followed by repentance and grief. Rinse and repeat. I did what I knew to do, when I didn't feel like it. I did it not because I wanted to, but because I knew I needed to. I did it because I could feel the chains of torment loosening a little more each time. I did it until I was free from the pain and free from unforgiveness. I could not let my deeply wounded heart become hard and brittle. Retreating behind walls of self-protection and throwing arrows of accusation was tempting. Letting everyone, everywhere, know who was to blame for my pain was tempting. But that was not the life I wanted to live. I could not get stuck here.

The journey out of the pit began with honesty about where I had lost trust in God. God promises never to leave or abandon me. Did I believe this? He says He will not let the waves take me under. Could I trust this? He proved Himself good and faithful over and over as I came to Him with crushing doubts, fears and pain, anger and hatred. He was there, guiding my story with life-infused words, weaving His love and grace into every moment.

We know how stories are written, and who the good Author is. We can trust God, and in doing so, our hearts begin to love and trust people again. Staying connected to God, who is able to work all things into something beautiful, keeps us moving forward with boldness and courage. And with soft, tender hearts.

I have always loved the imagery that John uses to introduce Jesus in the first pages of his gospel: "The Word gave life to everything that was created, and his life brought light to everyone. The light shines in the darkness, and the darkness can never extinguish it" (John 1:4–5).

John describes Jesus as God's Word to humanity. The Word gives light and life. The Word cannot be overpowered by the darkest night, or the crushing of death. And we are invited to partner with Him as we write our story.

To write brave, bold stories, we must refuse to put walls around our hearts. We must decide to pick up our pens and let hope flow onto our pages, even as the stories of others bump painfully into ours. To trust is to risk. To risk looking foolish. To risk being hurt. To risk going under completely in the next storm. Can we trust God to be faithful and good through every storm we encounter? Is God faithful when people lie, cheat, and steal? We are not hurt or punished or betrayed by God, but by those whom He would invite us to love. What if our stories are not made beautiful in spite of pain, but because of it? As I wrote in a journal entry,

> *Jesus is "near the broken-hearted" and comforts the warrior-heart: those who, in the midst of their pain and brokenness, posture themselves and say, "Love will win." Humbly crying out to God while fighting to keep their hearts tender, whole, and loving.*

- TWELVE -
At the Crossroads

When we are in pain, we have a great opportunity to grow in our thinking and capacity, shifting our lives for the better. We also have the temptation to escape what we have faced, reducing our lives day by day as we remain stuck.

I've met many people over the years who started out full of vision, purpose, dreams, and goals. But they stopped short of the life that could have been. Life got hard. Betrayal, abuse, or loss came, and they didn't know how to move forward. We will all have events in our journey that attempt to rob us of our confidence, joy, vision, and courage. We will all get knocked down by life. Why do some rise up and overcome, while others stop shy of the next adventure? Do you find yourself stuck? Waiting for someone to give you permission to continue, to rescue you from the pain?

Life has battles to be faced. Will we run toward the battle, or retreat into the safety of what is known?

Life is also full of success and beauty, tempting us to settle in comfortably as we stop wondering, *What else could there be on this journey*? It's up to each of us to keep going, trusting God's goodness as we press through the discomfort of change. What must shift in our thinking to get us unstuck? How do we step toward the promise God intends for us?

There's a story in the Bible that has bothered me for some time. A man named Abraham heard God, followed God, trusted God, and is called the father of the Christian faith. He was called to leave behind the land of his father's people for a land God had in mind. Yet it is Abraham's father, Terah, who has me stumped. Terah had three sons: Abram, Nahor, and Haran. The account in Genesis 11:31–32 lets us know that Haran died, leaving behind a son, Lot:

> One day Terah took his son Abram, his daughter-in-law Sarai (his son Abram's wife), and his grandson Lot (his son Haran's child) and moved away from Ur of the Chaldeans. He was headed for the land of Canaan, but they stopped at Haran and settled there. Terah lived for 205 years and died while still in Haran.

At first, it seems that Terah is on a mission. He picks up what's left of his family to move to Canaan. But they don't make it. Terah stops short and lives out the rest of his days in Haran.

I have long wondered if it was Terah who first heard the call to go to the land God promised. Is it possible that he started out in that direction, but got stuck on the way forward? Stuck in the pain of losing his son? Stuck in disappointment or fear?

Betrayal crashing into my life left me gasping for air, stopping me in my tracks. A single traumatic event, a season of suffering, or a lifetime of pain can cause us to get stuck.

Have we also settled in a land we were not meant for?

The meaning of the name *Haran* is "road, path, junction of trading routes, cross-roads."[1] Life guarantees that we will all come to intersections. When presented with various ways to proceed, what will guide us? Will pain dictate our next steps, or will love and vision guide the way?

Everyday Torment

I felt crazy. *Why am I reacting this way to such a small situation?* I asked myself. I was walking from my office to the coffee shop a block away, which had me on high alert for much longer than I want to admit. I felt that I wasn't safe and needed to watch for danger. Betrayal had imprinted on my heart and mind fear, humiliation, and anxiety. All the alarms were going off, telling me I wasn't safe, when in fact I was. I was on the lookout for certain types of vehicles, and any sign of people who reminded me of the betrayal. I never ran into anyone on my "coffee lap" who was actually a threat to my marriage, safety, or confidence. The torment in my soul was far worse than my reality.

I walked this path for months, the fear slowly subsiding. My heart lifted a prayer one day as I crossed the street: *God, please help me. I am so tired of living like this.*

I heard God's question in my mind, *What are you afraid of?*

I looked around, seeing clearly for the first time in far too long the short, one-mile stretch of Main Street. Shops, tourists, familiar faces of long-time locals. Coffee shops and restaurants with dogs waiting for their owners outside. *What was I afraid of?* I was afraid of humiliation, confrontation, and comparison. These words sum up the images of the horrible things I envisioned happening in the half-mile walk to and from the coffee shop.

God reminded me of all that I had come through and survived. No person, no situation could take me out. I had faced all the things I was afraid of, and had not backed down. I had made it this far, and would never be the same. I had grown. There was nothing to fear, even if I had to repeat the whole situation again. I was okay. I would be okay. In this moment with God my perspective shifted, and fear lifted.

Fully Present to the Past

What had happened was done, and was no longer happening. I didn't need to be on high alert for danger anymore. Yet being fully present to my life was a struggle for quite some time. Trauma wants to keep us stuck in the past, while we look for danger in our future. This leaves us missing the beautiful moments of today.

We are designed to be present, connected, and creative. I had to learn to shift my focus, and pull myself back into the reality of *this moment*—intentionally being present when my girls told me a story, while eating dinner, or playing a game.

While struggling to be present, I found ways to escape. Opening my work email or scrolling social media became addictions. It felt safe to be productive and distracted. It felt easier to escape the threat of memories that came while being still and present, rather than address the real issues head on. Interestingly, the better a present moment was, the faster I jumped to recycling pain on repeat in my mind.

I would often ask God, *Will I ever feel normal again? Will I ever be okay again?*

The answer, ultimately, was *Yes!* I can now walk around confidently in this small town filled with people who may or may not know our story. I continue to grow at being present with my friends and family. I am at peace. I am not afraid. I do not feel as though I am in constant danger.

Memories and Flashbacks

Another place I found myself stuck was in the good memories. Facebook would show "one year ago today" reminders of a happy, smiling family outing. Was this real? It felt like a big, fat lie. Could I hold onto a fun family memory, now knowing what had been happening deep below the surface?

Lysa TerKeurst, in her book *Forgiving What You Can't Forget*, gives us permission to choose which memories we keep, which we set on the shelf for a while, and which ones we pitch. Good memories do not need to be poisoned by current pain. When I found myself fixated on a memory that I thought was good, but was now clouded with lies and humiliation, I could choose to store it away in a shoebox under the bed, so to speak. Some memories I had to trust *were real*. Even in the midst of all that was going on, I could trust that this snapshot was real. We were a family, doing things together and enjoying each other's company.

The alternative was to believe that nothing was real and nothing was as it seemed. There are some memories and moments I did let go of. And some I only stashed away for a season. Most of these memories can now be taken out and looked at with the sting gone. Yes, it's true that things weren't as they should have been, but it was still a good memory, a good day in the midst of the shadows. Potentially, a moment that kept Duncan hanging on as long as he did. A moment that helped me remember what we were fighting for.

Then there were the evil, raw, crushing images and thoughts. The movies that played over and over. Images and scenes I hadn't actually witnessed, but what imagination had filled in. I would wake up with my mind racing, heart pounding, tears streaming at the overwhelming weight of them. These, too, had to be faced.

I knew that while my emotions were real, they weren't always reflecting current reality. They felt so real. Emotions can take us into a time and place that no longer exist, while lying to us about what's good today.

> *I asked Jesus to show me what was real,
> and to give me His lens of redemption to
> see through.*

I did my best to look for reality amidst the assumptions and fears. I asked Jesus to show me what was real, and to give me His lens of redemption to see through. I did my best to unravel the motives I had assigned to those who hurt me, and to see from God's perspective, though my view was blurry and clouded by my emotions. I would catch glimpses of wounded souls and broken hearts, not malicious and evil people.

I found a place of peace by being intentional. I found freedom through the practical, spiritual, and scientific practices that I am sharing with you in these pages, so you too can be wholly, beautifully free!

The Map to God's Promise

Have you ever taken a road trip with kids? Kids don't have a solid concept of time, making a long trip in a car feel endless. Outside their normal routine of going to school or the playground, they don't have familiar landmarks to track the progress of the trip. They just see the back of Mom and Dad's heads, and the road whizzing by.

"Are we there yet? When will we be there?"

My girls learned early on that there were some magic words they could speak that would bring the car to a quick stop along the side of the road. For our oldest, these magic words were "I have to go potty." When we were on a car trip, the portable potty seat came along in the trunk. At the time, we drove a Subaru Outback with a hatchback. Our daughter would sit contentedly on the potty seat, enjoying the Colorado views from the back of the car.

I remember on one trip we made it a mere fifteen miles outside of town before these words were dropped. I could only laugh as cars zoomed by, probably neighbors and colleagues from our small mountain town, wondering, W*haaattt?* Rarely was there an actual need that warranted the stop. What our daughter really wanted was to take a break, see our faces, and reorient herself in the world. But when you're potty training a kid, you stop the car. Are we much different in our pursuit of God in the midst of pain? Life seems to be zooming by in a dizzying blur, while we look frantically for something familiar and safe. It's different when we have the map and know the route, when we are in control. It's much harder to be heading somewhere we've never been, without the map, relying on a friend to get us to our destination.

This journey to freedom will require that we leave behind what is known. This is terrifying. For many, pain and distrust are the known factors. We know the game; we know the rules. Why would we hand over the keys and strap into the passenger seat without all the details for what's ahead? Especially after being wounded deeply. The unknown ahead cannot promise freedom, and remaining where we are certainly won't provide it. At least staying where we are—even if we remain stuck—is known.

Walking with Jesus is surrendering the map to Him. Today is a place that we are only meant to go through, not stay stuck in. We must look up, look ahead, and trust that God has the map, that He knows the way forward, that He has walked this way already, and that He has made a way through everything we will encounter.

Some people stay stuck. Others attempt to run from the pain. Running from pain brings more trouble, not less, as we seek anything and everything to become numb. Instead, we are invited to trust God's promise and to run *into* His goodness. Running *to* God means we can walk through life's messes and brokenness, and face it all head on, while becoming whole.

This is what it means to be an overcomer. To choose to pursue God and be transformed, no matter what our circumstances. We live in the tension of trusting God as we step into the unknown, writing the future while not knowing what awaits us around the next bend.

The truth is, I wanted an escape button. God didn't give me one. I don't think one exists. Instead, I was invited to walk through trials boldly. As I focused on Jesus, the old patterns and thought processes fell away. My faith was refined, and I became an overcomer.

So can you. It will mean facing some fears and honestly answering God's question, *What are you afraid of?* It will mean processing through some memories, and perhaps shelving others for now. It will mean choosing to see your current reality in the midst of emotions that want to overrun what's good today. It will mean, ultimately, handing the map to the One who already knows your future, and strapping into the passenger seat on this journey to becoming whole.

- THIRTEEN -
Purpose in the Pain

A broken heart feels incurable. The wounds inflicted are nothing short of irrational and unfair. Suffering doesn't look at resumes or merits to determine who is chosen. As questions swirled in my head, heart, and body, I begged God, *Please don't let all of this pain be for nothing. Please let there be a purpose.*

Writing that out now feels a bit odd. Why would I need to find a purpose for this pain? I couldn't explain it, but knowing that one day something valuable would come from this was needed for me to keep moving forward.

Pain in our body alerts us when something is wrong. That is its purpose. Pain in our souls functions the same way. Pain lets us know that something is broken or damaged, be it trust, identity, connection, or a dream. Pain isn't the problem; it's just the warning system that something deep inside us is out of place. We are in real danger when we can no longer feel pain.

To heal, we need more than knowledge of what is wrong. Meaning in suffering helps us see beyond the pain to what could be, and reminds us that our life is more than our experience. A cut by a skilled surgeon to remove disease is pain with meaning. A broken heart from the senseless and selfish choices of others is harder to bring meaning to. But God can show us that meaning, even when we can't see it for ourselves.

The truth I discovered in the process of overcoming betrayal was that Duncan's choices didn't *cause* me fear of abandonment, insecurity about my worth, or a sense of rejection in my soul. Those issues were already residing quietly and mostly dormant deep within. Betrayal *amplified* what was already within me.

I've heard stories of people injured in car accidents who were rushed to the hospital. While treating these people for the immediate trauma, doctors discovered a deeper, life-threatening issue. A disease not caused by the accident, but revealed by it, silently killing them from the inside out. If not for the accident, they would have died. This is how my journey feels. The broken places in my heart were going to suffocate me eventually. I kept pushing them off, trying to ignore them. Subtle but deadly fears of real intimacy, rejection, and abandonment were keeping me in bondage. The harmful lies tied to these fears kept me from confronting the deeper issues affecting my life and marriage. Yet life has a way of helping to keep us from slowly killing ourselves.

Overcome Despite the Pain

We are designed to overcome. Warriors rise up in the face of battles. If we believe our pain is meaningless, we won't seek God and cry out for the wisdom and grace to rise to the challenge ahead of us.

I have more of a rebellious streak than I'd like to admit. When someone says I can't do something, my first thought is, *Watch me*. I dare anyone to limit me with his or her fears. So when faced with pain and disappointment, I found myself looking at it as a challenge. When betrayal screams that I am unloved, broken, and should shut my heart off, I shout back, *I am the beloved daughter of God, made new every day and created for real love and intimacy! Just watch me overcome!*

I pray this same determination would rise in you also. To overcome, you and I must discover what we're willing to fight for. We need to believe that we are worthy and take our place on the battlefield. Are we willing to fight to become whole, so our children can have a healthy and connected parent? Can we chose to fight for a healed marriage, so our children don't have to experience the pain of a broken family?

How we choose to respond in suffering will determine if we overcome, or if we remain stranded in suffering. Will we become a victim, or a victor? Will we choose love and joy, or resentment and unforgiveness? Will we choose life, or death? I could not blame the "car accident" of our broken relationship for the "cancer" of fear already in my soul. I had to own the depravity already at work in me, and *rejoice* that these deeper issues had been revealed so I could face them.

Suffering . . . can have a meaning, if it changes you *for the better.*

Overcoming is not about making it through pain. Overcoming is growing despite pain, to become stronger, healthier, and more whole versions of ourselves. We can push back, and fight for our hearts to stay soft and full of love. Hope shows us what could be. Hope is what will guide us to finding the meaning in suffering that we are looking for. As one Holocaust survivor said, "Suffering . . . can have a meaning if it changes *you* for the better."[1]

My heart was broken and hurting, but I had to trust God not only to set things right from the betrayal, but also to cut me open and remove the cancerous lies and fears deep within my soul.

A Future beyond the Battle

I had a glimmer of hope that maybe, just maybe, choosing love over revenge, and reconciliation over justice, would bring about the change Duncan and I had needed for a long time. The stakes were high. Would we become another co-parenting, every-other-weekend statistic? If so, would I continue to trust that God would make it all good, even if it wasn't the outcome that I hoped for?

I couldn't always see what good could come from this mess, but I did my best to trust God. I allowed Him to show me where I was angry and afraid. I chose each day to pick up my mat and take a few tentative steps further from the bondage of the lies and strategies trying to keep hope at bay.

The reality of our broken marriage, and where our family was heading, were not what I had imagined when I said "*I do.*" I looked into the faces of our two sweet girls and knew that they deserved so much more. Words like *co-parenting*, *shared custody*, *separation*, and *divorce* were now in my vocabulary. When we got married, I had determined that divorce would never be an option. I believed that there wasn't anything we couldn't figure out. How could I hold on to that, especially when I only had 50 percent of the vote?

We don't overcome pain and suffering; we overcome in spite of them. Pain is the gift that tells us when something is not as it should be. This gives us the ability to figure out why, and how to adjust. Healing comes as we lay our souls before God, allowing His love to purge and cleanse and mend every broken thing.

Meaning comes when we trust that the battles we face will one day help another. As Charles Spurgeon reportedly said, pain, if sanctified, creates tenderness towards others. Meaning helps us walk through pain, knowing that our thoughts, words, and actions will resonate in eternity. Even in death, we can plant seeds of life. Our words and actions have power, and how we walk through our darkest moments does matter. Meaning helps us stay anchored to hope. Hope keeps us looking toward a future beyond the battle.

In our story, our girls were an anchor that kept us holding on. We could do better, we could heal, we could grow and give ourselves, and our marriage, the chance we never had . . . for them. I know we both held onto hope and fought harder for our marriage because these beautiful girls deserved more than our brokenness. Whether we stayed together or separated, we knew we had a lot of work to do to give them that.

Dream, but Don't Fixate

The essence of hope is being able to imagine and move toward a future better than our current reality. When we have experienced trauma, this can be difficult. Not because we don't want to do it, or because we aren't trying. But the force of the trauma physically impacts our brains, and we need help to imagine and dream again. Without imagination, there's no hope. Those who experience the blunt-force impact of a car accident are not expected to recover immediately from the physical trauma. So why do we expect ourselves or others to get over a broken heart quickly? I have discovered that trauma of any kind (whether injury to body or soul) requires both emotional and physical healing.

How do we begin to heal these soul wounds and move forward? I love how Dr. Bessel van der Kolk in *The Body Keeps the Score* describes the importance of imagination in producing hope:

> Imagination is absolutely critical to the quality of our lives. Our imagination enables us to leave our routine everyday existence by fantasizing about travel, food, sex, falling in love, or having the last word—all the things that make life interesting. Imagination gives us the opportunity to envision new possibilities—it is an essential launchpad for making our hopes come true. It fires our creativity, relieves our boredom, alleviates our pain, enhances our pleasure, and enriches our most intimate relationships. When people are compulsively and constantly pulled back into the past, to the last time they felt intense involvement and deep emotions, they suffer from

a failure of imagination, a loss of the mental flexibility. Without imagination there is no hope, no chance to envision a better future, no place to go, no goal to reach.[2]

Meaning and hope are linked. Hope says, *There is a better future ahead, and the suffering we cannot emotionally or mentally make sense of can one day have meaning.* Those who've been abused may envision opening a shelter for women so others can escape the nightmare. Those mourning the loss of a loved one may dream of finding meaningful ways of serving others as a way to honor their friend or family member.

The one condition for hope is that we cannot become fixated on a specific outcome. If we attach our happiness and healing to a certain outcome, we will face disappointment and more pain if, and likely when, that outcome doesn't unfold exactly the way we decided it must in order for us to be okay.

I could dream about having a great marriage, while also hoping for a good future, a faithful, loving husband, and freedom from the pain of betrayal—whether or not Duncan was part of it. As I mentioned earlier, sometimes my prayers were for "my husband," rather than Duncan specifically. I wanted that person to be Duncan. But fixating on a specific outcome would have moved my prayers and actions from hope and love to control and manipulation. I could feel the draw to these forces that were fear based, not love birthed. When we are dead set on how things should be, we will fall into this trap of control and manipulation. These are strategies of evil, not love. We cannot afford to fall for this lesser version of hope. Our hope is in Jesus, no matter the outcome. As we rest in His presence and seek to know Him, we will be filled with faith for the best outcome. We will be able to choose love, no matter what it may look like when we get there.

At the same time, I did pray for Duncan, and I declared a reality that wasn't yet visible. I prayed that *Duncan was a man of integrity and faithfulness, a man who loved God and led his family in truth.*

This is a tricky tension to be in. To walk in love for those who have hurt us, and pray boldly for the best outcomes—while simultaneously not getting attached to having the circumstances turn out a specific way. A subtle, but powerful temptation for me was holding too tightly to what I envisioned that repair and repentance should look like. The real signs were subtle, and often not what I expected. I had to choose to accept these small, humble, and easy-to-miss signs that our marriage was healing. The best we can do when navigating these rough waters is to hold Jesus tightly and our future loosely, knowing that He is good and will bring good to us, often in unexpected ways. Unhealthy attachments to our expectations for *one day* can cause us to miss the progress we have made *this day*.

Whether our situation resolves the way we hope or not—reconciled or estranged, healed on earth or healed in heaven—the tools that will help us heal are the same. The good that God can bring to our circumstances isn't determined by getting this just right, or by other people making the choices we hope they'll make. Those who desired reconciliation but found their marriage ending, those who stayed, those who prayed for life but planned a funeral, those who believed for breakthrough but found more broken pieces—they can all find freedom and healing, and even purpose in it all.

The good that can arise from senseless pain and loss will unravel over time. God sees you and is in the business of creating *beauty from ashes* (see Isaiah 61:1–3). Every weapon sent to destroy you will become powerful in your hand to wield in defense of others. You are not alone in this journey. Please don't lose heart, don't give up. We need you, dear warrior, to find your strength and take your place on the battlefield.

Maybe that's why I am writing this book. I have struggled deeply with telling you this story. It really isn't anyone's business. But if it sets someone free, it will have been worth it. I will wield this story as an anthem of overcoming grace, so you can pick it up and find hope in your story.

Who will be waiting for you on the other side of your mess? Who will be needing desperately the wisdom and grace you have fought for along the way?

Are you ready to let go of what was, and begin to ask God to show you what could be? Declare over your circumstances today that *God is working all things together for good.*

- FOURTEEN -
"Why, God?"

Let's be honest—life isn't fair. If God could stop the storm, why didn't He? It would be easy to conclude that He is unwilling, unable, or finds me unworthy. Many wounded warriors have been lost to these questions.

As a mom, I often struggle with the tension of keeping my kids safe while allowing them to take healthy risks. The message seems to be that good parents diligently protect children from every pointy, sharp, and potentially harmful object. By removing risk, we remove problem-solving and growth. The normal childhood dangers of tree climbing, pond swimming, and neighborhood romping build creativity and strength.

Instead of equipping children to climb mountains, we hover and wait, ready to helicopter them out of the avalanche of the mean kid's words or the landslide of a poor grade on a test. We hand out *"Be careful"* and *"Stay safe"* more than *"I trust you"* and *"You've got this."* Has this informed our view of how we believe God should show up for us?

Growing up in a world where we're taught that a good parent swoops in at the onset of any and all discomfort leaves us swirling in the wreckage of life, wondering where our helicopter rescue was.

Where were you, God?

Pain blinds us to the good around us. We cannot see God's movements in the dark, but are left trusting until we get to the other side that *He will never leave or abandon us.*

> Let your character or moral disposition be free from love of money [including greed, avarice, lust, and craving for earthly possessions] and be satisfied with your present [circumstances and with what you have]; for He [God] Himself has said, I will not in any way fail you nor give you up nor leave you without support. [I will] not, [I will] not, [I will] not in any degree leave you helpless nor forsake nor let [you] down (relax My hold on you)! [Assuredly not!]
> Hebrews 13:5 AMPC[1]

A Strand of Pure Gold

When I was feeling gut-punched by what had happened in our marriage, God showed me a picture as I cried out to Him. My prayers at any given moment could be a mix of anger, fear, hope, trust, and questions. I could pray powerfully one moment, cowering in the corner with my fears the next. My heart and mind were trying to put all the pieces together, to make the pain make sense. God painted in my mind an image of a beautiful tapestry. Some threads were frayed, and some were still loose and in the process of being woven into place. One thread caught my eye, a beautiful strand of pure gold, being woven from beginning to end in this ever-evolving tapestry. The golden line was holding parts of the tapestry together, pulling new parts into the image and making it all beautiful.

God was showing me where He is in my story—in the beginning, and at the end. Weaving and winding, creating and healing as He pulls all the pieces together, no matter how frayed or tattered they become. He is always working to make my life look more like Jesus.

Still, my heart often asked, *Why, God?* I logically understand why bad things happen. I theologically understand why bad things happen. And I don't blame God. Yet the heart of this question for me was, *God, I did all of the things a good Christian girl does. Isn't there some special exemption or protection from suffering, for my devotion?*

Maybe you've asked a version of this question too. We aren't really asking *Why, God?* But *Why ME, God? Why did I have to be the one to suffer?*

When I look at the terrible suffering some people have overcome, I find a common thread: They had meaning and purpose beyond the pain. When our suffering feels irrational and meaningless, we must look outside the circumstances to remember that our life does have meaning and that God promises He will work all the things into something good. The meaningless, the senseless, the horrific, it can all be entrusted to God to be woven into something meaningful, beautiful, and full of life.

> **The meaningless, the senseless, the horrific, it can all be entrusted to God to be woven into something meaningful, beautiful, and full of life.**

I found meaning as I was able to see God's heart for Duncan. I saw in my husband a heart that was hurting, had given up on just about everything, and needed love. And I was in the right place at the right time to bring God's love. This was a rescue mission for a man's heart. God gave me an unreasonable grace in reminding me day after day that I was fighting for something important. God showed me His heart toward Duncan, and that this really was a rescue mission. I decided that I was not a victim, and would not take the bait of getting stuck in such a powerless mindset. I was powerful to love, no matter what others would chose.

A Deep Well of Healing

Please don't hear me say that I'm the hero. This is still real life, with real choices, pain, and failure. We failed our way through the first thirteen years of our marriage. We were now trying to decide how to—or if to—move forward together. We made many more mistakes along the way. But we both kept showing up, trying to do better and repair our marriage. Duncan demonstrated real repentance and chose to open his heart to me, even when it was really, really hard for both of us. There also were still boundaries needing to be set, and very real consequences that had to be addressed.

If you listen to God's answer to the *Why me?* questions, you might hear *Because I needed a warrior who would choose love.* Love that would walk away if needed, and love that would stay if asked. Love that would serve, love that would speak the truth, love that would confront lies and battle evil strategies, love that would comfort, love that would bring healing. Whatever real and true love was needed in a moment, God knew you would deliver it from His heart into the painful situation confronting you.

Maybe not now, or not yet, but one day life will come from what you overcome. If you choose love and keep your heart soft toward God, the transformation and beauty that will flow out of you will be a deep well of healing for others. My deeper connection to Jesus, and the transformation that I have gained in this process, have far outweighed the season of pain and suffering I endured. It can be so for you, too.

I don't want to neglect to repeat that sometimes real love means walking away from a relationship with those we love. If you are in a situation where abuse, betrayal, or lies continue without a change of heart or behavior, loving well may mean creating a safe distance or setting healthy boundaries. It may potentially mean stepping away from the relationship. We need wisdom, guidance, and godly counsel to navigate these issues.

Stepping Out, Sword Swinging

The next question I wrestled with was, *Didn't God let me down by not protecting me from the harm I endured?* I mean, *He allowed this*, right?

God entrusted this world to humanity. The evil we experience is what *we* have allowed. We allow evil to wreak havoc when we disobey God, when we choose unforgiveness, gossiping, or lies. Evil creeps in when we are selfish or partner with arrogance and pride. People make choices every day to allow love or hate, goodness or evil, fear or peace, into this world through their attitudes and actions.

Even in all the pain and chaos in the world, God has equipped us with what is needed to overcome and to bring life in the face of death. (I will go into this in more detail in chapter 23, "Fire Forged.")

Where were you, God? is another question I asked. I knew the answer, but it wasn't enough. Why are we surprised when life is hard? It's as if we are looking for an exemption from being human. Deep down, the question *Where were you, God?* is our heart asking *Am I safe*? If my most intimate partner could wound me so deeply, where am I safe? Was God intervening in ways I didn't know and couldn't see? Or is He an aloof father figure, kind, but unmoved by my circumstances?

I asked, and God answered. He knew a test was coming, and He reminded me that I had been enrolled in school without my realizing it. God didn't write the test. He knew Duncan's choices were going to cut my heart open, revealing everything deep within, revealing the strength of my faith, hope, and love. The answers to the questions in this test would determine where my trust really was. God had been tutoring me day by day for several years. He had been giving me lessons on being powerful and learning to forgive, and teaching me the principles of loving well. And now I got to put these lessons to the test.

While my questions still echoed in the darkness, I knew that I had been prepared for this moment. Preparation didn't make it easier, but it equipped me to step onto the battlefield and face the lies, fear, and insecurity that were coming against me, our marriage, and our family. There really wasn't any other choice I wanted to make. I didn't know if I would win or lose. I just knew I had to step out, sword swinging, and give it all I had.

At the local gym, a young man from our community was training for a competitive sporting event. This young man always says what's in his head, loud and clear, for everyone to hear. And he is one of the most encouraging and positive people I've ever met. I was within earshot as he was doing an arm workout with his coach, and I overheard him lament, "It just gets harder every time I do it!"

I laughed and told him, "Me too!"

I often tell my girls that it's okay to be uncomfortable, to push our bodies to be stronger. Pain isn't bad. Pain now in the gym will get that young man across the finish line of his event. Pain now in discipline will move us forward exponentially when it matters in the battle. Don't take for granted or be discouraged by the equipping God is doing within you. It will get you across the finish lines you can't yet see.

- FIFTEEN -
Overcoming Doubt

There are serious implications to doubting God. Questions don't have to lead to doubt. We can question God, tell Him how we really feel, and still find deep in our hearts a belief that He is good. Questions can allow us to see the condition of our heart, and they can allow God to respond.

Doubt, however, waits to creep in and steal trust. Fear raises questions not about God's ability in the storm, but about His nature. The lie creeps in slowly as we swim to shore, windbeaten, waterlogged, and coughing up seaweed: *Maybe God isn't good.*

How we view God will determine how, and even if, we overcome. There are many times I have had to do a heart check to see where my trust *really* is. Am I believing in a specific outcome more than believing in God no matter where the circumstances land?

Surviving the storm but staying stuck in the wreckage, we can fall prey to strange doctrines that tell us God must hurt us to help us. Confusing punishment with discipline leaves many wondering, *Why would I trust a God like that?* You can't, and shouldn't, trust someone who brings destruction or evil and declares, *"It was for your good!"* That is manipulation and abuse, and

God's ways are higher. Much higher.

Others who are in pain decide, *This is just the way it is*. And settle for a life devoted to great doctrines of knowledge without power. Giving up, often little by little, on what they once pursued so passionately. Settling for a life of passive perseverance rather than fighting for overcoming faith. Sticking it out, remaining stuck. Waiting for a rescue. Knowledge doesn't win battles. The truth we say we believe must be tested on the battlefield.

Wrong Questions Keep You Stuck

Why? and *What if?* questions don't play fair. They leave us stuck in the past, instead of looking toward Jesus and a hope-filled future. They lure us into imagining a past without pain and a future of ease and comfort. These questions are void of hope, portraying a future that is dependent on a perfect past.

We don't have authority in the past. We don't have the capacity to take care of tomorrow's problems today. We only have authority and grace for this day—not yesterday, or tomorrow. Hope looks to a future that is not yet here, deals with the fallout of what happened yesterday, and stands firm in God's love and grace today. Look back to heal and address your wounded soul, and look ahead with hope, while living fully present in this day.

Instead of asking God where He was when the waves were crashing, ask yourself, *Where was my attention in the storm?* It might be that God is at work in ways we can't see because we are looking only at what was wrong. Trusting that God is good will focus our attention on how He has shown up, is showing up, and will show up with life and power in every situation we encounter.

One more question that plagues us is, *Whose fault is this?* Jesus encounters a man born blind, and His disciples have some interesting questions for Him: "Rabbi," the disciples ask, "why was this man born blind? Was it because of his own sins or his parents' sins?" (John 9:2). Hebrew culture held the promise that those who followed God's ways would be healthy, whole, and successful. Those who were not must be cursed. Blindness was a debilitating disability, leaving a person utterly helpless in society.

Some scholars link the Old Testament rule of "an eye for an eye" with punishment for sinning against another.[1] Surrounding cultures held the view that blindness was a curse, and blinding someone would be used as a means to control prisoners of war.

The assumption the disciples are making is that this man's blindness is a consequence for sins, whether his parents' or his own. The disciples are asking a question in line with their culture, *Who's sin is he being punished for?* Yet I find it interesting that there are so many others walking around in this story with perfect eyesight. Had no one else in this community ever chosen death over life?

Your Bible translation of Jesus' response may read, ""It was not because of his sins or his parents' sins. . . . This happened so the power of God could be seen in him" (John 9:3). Yet the words *This happened so* are not in the original text. A better translation is *But*, or *Nevertheless*. The word used to transition between *Who's at fault here?* and *the power of God* is a Greek word, *alla*, that can be translated *but, nevertheless, howbeit, therefore*.[2] This word creates *an objection* in the Greek,[3] dividing between the disciples' question and God's nature.

This is an important place to pause and dive into the truth of Jesus' words. Does God orchestrate bad things in our life to bring about good? Are people born blind so God can get the glory for their healing? The disciples are saying (my paraphrase), "Clearly this is punishment for someone's sins! Who's to blame?" I know I have asked similar questions.

Jesus responds (again my paraphrase), "NO! This is not punishment for sin. It's just part of a broken world. BUT! Let's get to work healing the sick and wounded so that God may be glorified!"

When bad things happen, we want someone or something to blame. Placing blame allows us to remain powerless to control how we respond to what happens to us. Blame says, *I'm a victim, and my offender deserves to be punished.* We think if there's someone to blame for our suffering, to throw the weight of it all on, then maybe we can be free. While there are punishments and consequences for partnering with evil, these aren't in our hands to distribute. Even if we could demand retribution, doing so would not mend the broken places in our soul.

The pernicious underbelly of blame is turning it on God. This says, *God needed to cause this illness or betrayal or loss so that I would turn toward Him.* I've been taught that Jesus is perfect theology. He is the perfect representation of God's heart and ways. I never find Jesus declaring sickness over someone, sending curses on people, or abusing them in any way to get them to turn toward Him or bring glory to the Father.

> **I've been taught that Jesus is perfect theology. He is the perfect representation of God's heart and ways.**

Don't get me wrong—I was angry. I was broken. Betrayal hurts like hell. I screamed into pillows, and on long drives. I cried and blamed and asked all the questions. But I've had too much experience with God and His unfailing goodness to believe that He orchestrated this betrayal. I knew I couldn't afford to confuse why this had happened with who God is. God has revealed Himself as faithful; therefore, betrayal is against His nature. God has revealed Himself as our Healer; therefore, sickness is against His nature. God has revealed Himself as the Life Giver; therefore, death is against His nature.

In the middle of what is not good, we can find the good and beautiful. Strength, joy and hope, healing and freedom will begin to work out of us as we turn toward God. God is just that good. He takes the worst of the worst and creates a better today than we could have imagined. God doesn't have to burn your life to the ground to show up as faithful and good. We just don't look for His goodness at work when life is comfortable. We don't cry out for miracles when we can charge the credit card or visit the doctor. When God is our only option, then we seem to find the miraculous. That's on us and our approach, not on God's willingness to show up today.

We can assign blame, or we can activate our faith for the assignment before us: to trust God, and to love people.

The Pity Party Trap

God told me clearly, *You cannot be the victim and be victorious.*

Suffering leads to grief, and grief can quickly turn into self-pity. Self-pity declares, *You are the victim; you are powerless, and someone else has to fix this for you.* But who will? No one else is coming to live your life and choose your freedom.

I *wanted* to be a victim, at least for a little bit. It would have been comforting to plaster social media with the injustices perpetrated against me. (*See! It's not my fault that I'm a raging, angry, exhausted, sobbing mess every day! Look what happened to me!*) It's false strength to engage in conversations that disintegrate into blame. We cannot win the battles in front of us by wielding the strategies of blame and accusation. An accusatory mindset prevents us from becoming truly powerful in the midst of pain. I knew I had to choose carefully whom I talked with and walked with. I couldn't afford to bring people into our story who would allow me to be a powerless victim.

Throwing a pity party might have made me feel good—momentarily. But it would have done far more harm than good to my hurting heart. It won't do your heart any good either.

The pity party trap is set. Will we choose to find comfort in telling everyone how bad we've had it, continuing to point blame for our suffering? Or will we find comfort in the Comforter and healing in the Healer who infuses us with the strength to become whole, love fully, and radiate life amidst the darkness?

Discipline vs. Punishment

Doesn't the Bible say that all discipline is good, and that I should accept it joyfully? (See Hebrews 12:5–11.) First, we need to distinguish between God's discipline and the evil in the world. They are not the same. Next, we need to distinguish between discipline and punishment. The goal of discipline is to teach us to choose what's good physically, emotionally, and spiritually.

Discipline communicates who we are, and who we aren't. Discipline reminds us that we are powerful, loving beings with the capacity to make healthy or unhealthy choices. The consequences speak for themselves when we go outside of boundaries that bring connection and life.

Discipline can be painful, but it doesn't cause death or destruction. In my life, I've found that obedience to Jesus can be painful. Like pulling a splinter, or doing a hard workout, the pain of obedience and discipline moves us toward life. Obedience means leaving behind wrong attitudes, humbly admitting mistakes, and repenting of my wrongdoing. This can hurt as my soul tries desperately to hold onto what I perceive keeps me safe, keeps me looking important, or keeps me in control.

Yet this process is completely different from punishment, or even the pain caused by others' choices. A verse I remind myself of in this process of obedience is James 1:21: "So get rid of all the filth and evil in your lives, and humbly accept the word God has planted in your hearts, for it has the power to save your souls." God does not need to employ evil to teach, train, or grow me. His words (both the words found in my Bible, as well as the whispers in my heart as I spend time with Him in prayer) have all the power necessary to bring life to my attitudes, thinking, and beliefs.

In contrast, punishment communicates that we are bad, and that when we make a wrong choice, someone steps in to make sure we know we did wrong. An abusive form of punishment is using manipulation to create the behavior we want others to conform to. This can be physical abuse, verbal abuse, or emotional and relational neglect. Yet God is never abusive in the way He deals with His children. Punishment for evil is a biblical reality, yet God does not employ this tactic as a means to teach or train His children. Punishment is for the unrepentant, those unwilling to change, be softened by love, or respond to God's reality.

Would you rather have love and discipline guiding you, or fear of punishment? If we believe that God is a punisher and the pain we experience is His guidance, we will not run to Him in the storms.

My definitions and observations here are based on being in relationships and experiencing the healthy dynamics of discipline, and the unhealthy dynamics of punishment. I've gone through subtle, yet powerful shifts in how I think about interacting with others, and seeing how God wants to interact with us. I hope this helps you shift your thinking, too, from victim to victorious, from blame placer to powerful and loving, from pity party planner to running to God in the storm. With God, I have never been abused or used. God has never punished me for making mistakes. He won't do that to you either. He is love, loves you intensely, and will help you love others, even the unlovable.

Love believes the best, and calls us higher. Human punishment assumes the worst, and uses control to conform others to an external version of good. Godly punishment protects people from the evil of others, and themselves. What He offers you and me is His protection, good discipline, grace, and strength in the storm. If we reach for Him and receive what He is offering, our *Why, God?* becomes *What now, God? Show me how to pass this heart test, and I'll do it. Because I know you'll love me through it, and help me choose to love others, for your glory . . .*

- SIXTEEN -
Emotions are Good

I have experienced faith communities that communicate subtly but powerfully that emotions are bad. Or at least the hard emotions. Radiating thankfulness, joy, and peace? Great! You must be doing something *right* and have lots of faith! Anxious, lonely, angry, confused, or disappointed? Well, friend, you need to memorize more Bible verses about thankfulness! Find that joy and peace!

We don't like seeing our friends in pain, so when someone grieves beyond our comfort level, we retreat from the hard conversations. Feeling powerless to help others overcome the pain they're experiencing, we say the dumbest things ever: "Just get over it; he has." "There are people who would love to have your problems." As if painful experiences have a ranking system that makes some better or worse than others.

In my pain, I often experienced very real and powerful emotions. In the blink of an eye, the flood threatened to take me under. I got to the point where there really wasn't anyone left who could help me navigate the surprising, all-encompassing waves. To be honest, I can understand how no one was interested in hearing me recount the same struggles, fears, and insecurities over and over. In suffering and grief, I needed people connected enough to their own humanity to sit with me and listen without going under with me. Friends could help me to a certain point, but I needed professional counsel to overcome the deepest parts of this wound.

Unfortunately, many do not move beyond the initial phase of compassion and empathy offered by friends, into true healing. Maybe you, too, have taken the advice of those unable to counsel you all the way through the deepest pain. Taking the well-meaning but extremely damaging advice to "just move past it," the overwhelming emotions and wounds still bleeding get buried deep down as we attempt to "just be more thankful and joyful."

I have heard for decades that Jesus followers should get their eyes off the problem and praise Jesus, no matter what's happening. This is 100 percent true—unless it's not. There are times when this advice isn't helpful in overcoming pain. Instead, it creates an atmosphere that encourages hurting people to ignore pain, causing more damage than good. Emotions feel like reality. Thoughts paint images of what was and will be with such force that they are difficult to escape.

Pray or Praise through Pain?

We need to become aware of what our real and raw emotions are trying to communicate to us. There are times to praise through pain. There are times to pray through pain. There are times to weep through pain. There are times to talk through the pain. And there are times to listen quietly through the pain. The goal is to get *through the pain*, with the Holy Spirit guiding the healing journey.

The most freeing words for suffering and grief that I've found are from the book of James. These words welcomed and gave solutions to the depth of pain I was experiencing: "Is anyone among you afflicted (ill-treated, suffering evil)? He should pray. Is anyone glad at heart? He should sing praise [to God]" (James 5:13 AMPC).

There were absolutely times when I could declare and rejoice over *what God was doing and what was to come*. These were powerful times when I could praise God for His goodness and love in the middle of the pit. There were also times when the dark emotions overwhelmed me, and I needed to address them. I don't believe we can praise away trauma. These words from the Bible state that we are to *pray* when we are suffering evil. Prayer for me is a deep, worshipful communion with Jesus, my Creator, Savior, and Lover. It's a space where I pour out my heart, and He pours out His. My heart releases poison, fear, anger, and pride. He releases love, power, and life into me. Until I pour out what's in me, there's no room for what He longs to fill me with.

Emotions signal to us and those around us that something is not okay within. They point to where we need healing. They let us know something is wrong. Imagine your *Check Engine* light coming on in your car and having a mechanic tell you, "Turn the radio up louder, and it will go away." Truly, the issue would go away eventually when the engine seized, and the car would be sent to the junkyard. A pure, believing heart must take the emotional warning lights seriously and without shame. Anger, fear, grief—these are signals that it's time to slow down, spend time in God's presence, and allow the flame of His love to reveal wounds, scar tissue, or infections lying deep within. And to *pray*. Talk to God about what you feel. Ask Him where the pain is coming from and how to address it.

Inviting Others to Meet Us Where We're At

Emotions also allow others to meet us in our story. The word *sympathy* comes from the Latin word *sympathia*[1] and encompasses feeling what others feel, and allowing what affects our friends to affect us. Emotions are not meant to separate us from each other. When shared and received, they bring comfort, connection, and healing. Do we view our emotions as assets that inform and bond us, or liabilities that are untrustworthy and evil?

Do we view our emotions as assets that inform and bond us, or liabilities that are untrustworthy and evil?

While we don't want to fall into the habit of constant navel-gazing, as I've heard Bill Johnson put it, there are times when we need to sit with God and get clarity on what's going on inside us. Are my emotions pointing to an area I need to renew my mind in, a lie I'm believing, an unhealed trauma, a spiritual agreement I've made that I need to repent of? I'm just not smart enough to figure this out on my own. I need discernment. I need God's help. And I need wise counselors and trained therapists to help me discover what's going on in my heart. There are also times we need to be brave, and invite, or maybe invite again, people to meet us where we are.

I am learning to be very curious about what I'm feeling. I ask myself, *Why do I feel anxious around that person or place? What is this overwhelming sense of sadness? What brings me peace and clarity? What brings me joy and refreshing?* A good counselor will help us dig below the surface of our emotions with curiosity, to help find the root of these emotions. Until we address what's at the core of our feelings, they will continue to cause damage.

It's not healthy to pretend we're okay when we're not. It's not okay to feel as if we're not allowed to experience negative emotions. It's not okay to be around toxic positivity that neglects genuine healing (more on that in a moment).

God is the Healer of both our bodies and our souls. Our soul is the place our emotions dwell. It can be broken and crushed, wounded and bleeding. Jesus binds up broken hearts, minds, and emotions. He wraps in love, soothes with healing balms, and carefully attends to the wounds we allow Him to access. It's the hard emotions that point us to the wounds that need the Healer.

We don't need to be ashamed of what we feel. Finding professional counselors to walk through the healing journey with us and address the emotions screaming for attention is vital.

Wise Counsel or Toxic Positivity?

Years ago, a man came to me for prayer. He had a very painful past and a slew of health issues. We talked and prayed. I gave him some steps to take. Not long after, I found him having the exact same conversation with another leader in our church, and expressing the exact same prayer request. His health issues never seemed to get better. His conversation never changed from what had happened, to what a future free of this ailment would look like.

There's a difference between seeking out those who can help us take the next step to freedom, and searching out someone new whom we can relive our story with as we seek validation and attention rather than healing. I pray that we would all ask God to show us our motives and deepest needs as we seek out counsel.

Wise counsel will help us see, name, and address what's going on inside our hearts and minds, bringing real freedom. It's okay to take your time with it, while also determining not to remain stuck in any pain or suffering. When we are genuinely seeking counsel that moves us toward healing, we will come across what has been coined *toxic positivity*. Those who follow Jesus might be the biggest culprits of this, but I'm not sure.

Proverbs 25:20 confused me, until I encountered toxic positivity in the middle of my pain: "When you sing a song of joy to someone suffering in the deepest grief and heartache, it can be compared to disrobing in the middle of a blizzard or rubbing salt in a wound" (TPT). Now when I read this verse, I can relate to someone who has been left exposed, vulnerable, and unsafe in the counsel of someone else who has little awareness of how to address the real needs of pain and suffering.

I mentioned earlier about the healing conference with Randy Clark. The worship team was small, simple, and powerful. They didn't start with the usual "clap your hands and praise" routine, as so many worship leaders are in the habit of doing. They kept it simple, kept their eyes on Jesus, and gently led the room into His presence. Within thirty seconds of the first song, I had tears streaming down my face. I had been on the battlefield for so long, fighting for my marriage, and dealing with triggers and trauma and hypervigilance to keep myself safe. Yet this felt like finding a cabin in the woods, where an old granny lived. She gently bathed, clothed, and fed me before putting me in the softest of beds to rest. I was safe. I could rest. I could heal. I didn't realize how much I needed the Comforter until this worship team led me to Him.

At the conference, we were a room full of broken and hurting people needing physical, mental, and emotional healing, and hoping for a touch from God. If the worship team had begun with upbeat praise music and had pushed to get the room excited, it would have hamstrung what the Holy Spirit wanted to do.

Why? Because beginning in that way would have put the responsibility on the people, as so many worship leaders do each weekend. Yes, we enter God's gates with thanksgiving. But is thanksgiving always expressed in upbeat, exuberant praise? Starting as a quiet whisper might also get you there.

Going through the Roof

I love the story in the Bible of the four friends who cut a hole in the roof of a house to get their paralyzed friend to Jesus (see Mark 2:1–12). The home was full and overflowing with people who were there to see Jesus and hear His words. Many in the crowd likely needed healing. Yet look at these friends take action: "They couldn't bring him to Jesus because of the crowd, so they dug a hole through the roof above his head" (verse 4).

We need to know when it's time to help each other through thanksgiving, and when it's time to lower a friend gently through the roof, into Jesus' arms for healing. Spoiler alert: Jesus loved this act of faith on the part of these four friends.

The idea of "entering with thanksgiving" sometimes feels as though I'm being told that *I can get myself there* . . . I can enter the courts of God in my own strength and power. This is not God's heart in giving us the choice to praise Him when we're hurting. Have we taken this powerful gift and turned it into a task to accomplish before being welcomed by the Father? The truth is, we can't do any of this in our own power. Entering His presence with a grieving, hurting soul sometimes takes being lowered through the roof of a house by your friends. Humble enough to realize you can't push through and get yourself there, except for a simple prayer: *Jesus, help.*

I was the crippled friend who couldn't press through the crowds to get close to Jesus. If upbeat, shouting, clapping praise had been the start to entering God's presence that day at the conference, I would have walked out. It would have been fake for me, and I was tired of pretending I was okay. I was exhausted.

Praise is warfare. Praise is good and tells our souls that we will exalt God above our circumstance. Yet we also need healing worship that invites the Comforter to tend to our wounds when we've been on the battlefield. As the team that weekend so carefully followed the Holy Spirit, I was tearfully, worshipfully, gratefully lowered to the feet of the Healer. I didn't have to work up anything; I just rested and trusted in His presence.

- SEVENTEEN -
Being Human

Have you ever prayed for God to take away negative, hard, painful emotions? While we can pray and worship and find our way to hope in Jesus, which does lift our spirits and heal our souls, it's not a one-and-done solution for hard, deeply painful emotions.

Many of my prayers, when all the pain of these ugly emotions arose, came down to *God, please fix this situation, and please fix me.*

Yet by asking God to remove the negative emotions, I was essentially asking Him to take away what makes me human. Instead of ignoring my humanity, the very parts of me that express His image to the world, God offered me a revelation of His love, goodness, and grace that is only found in the deepest valleys.

Jesus promises to hold us together when grief tears us apart. Jesus experienced the real and raw reality of being human: Jesus wept. Jesus was angry. Jesus is jealous for us. Jesus speaks the truth in love. He is grieved by the choices people make. Yet Jesus is *without sin*.

We can feel deeply, even grieve deeply, without stepping out of love. In

Ephesians 4:26, Paul says, "Don't sin by letting anger control you." Paul is exhorting us not to let anger stay too long, because holding onto the negative opens the door to more evil, and to a life without love.

Be angry, and do not sin. Grieve, and do not sin. Desire, love, have ambition, and do not sin. Have mental, emotional, and physical needs, and do not sin. Have compassion, and do not sin. We can feel even the most painful emotions deeply while refusing to assign motives, make accusations, or gossip about those who have hurt us. We sin in our emotions when we begin to self-protect, justify, and try to meet our heart's needs on our own terms.

Where Are Your Emotions Taking You?

We need to feel emotions without allowing them to take over our lives. Emotions are real, yet they do not always reflect reality. We can feel deeply as we recall something that happened in the past. But as long as we ignore the emotional cues in our soul, we will not be free. Until we are free, we are susceptible to being emotion-led, not Spirit-led.

I find it interesting that within the word *emotion* is *motion*. "E-motions" take us somewhere. They can carry us to a place we may not want to be. They can also move us toward healing, when acknowledged and addressed.

Until we release the emotional pain of yesterday, we cannot step into the new season before us.

Ignoring negative emotions creates an internal world where darkness can take root. Holding onto pain through ignoring it, stuffing it, or remaining a victim to it grants access and authority for evil and torment to move into our hearts and lives. To find freedom, we must lean into what our "e-motions" are revealing about the wounds in our souls. As our brokenness is brought into the light, the Holy Spirit will provide wisdom for each step into wholeness.

There's a difference between not allowing emotions to control us and ignoring emotions. When we ignore, criticize, or minimize our very real emotions, we are ignoring part of what it means to be human. Growing up in church, I've watched many God-fearing churchgoers ignore the hard parts of being human. Rather than turning to vices such as drugs, alcohol, or entertainment to soothe our pain, we overspiritualize it. We know pain and suffering isn't the way life was meant to be. Rather than looking at why we are experiencing such overwhelming feelings, we have learned to stuff them, ignore them, and keep them hidden. This doesn't create motion; it creates stagnation. The pain festers and burns internally, creating a putrid internal world that eventually spills out around us.

Acknowledging feelings and being curious about what we are feeling invites new perspectives as our emotions are brought into the light and love of Jesus. I've found that when I'm angry, if I will sit and look deeper into what's going on in my heart, I will find deep sadness that I haven't paid attention to. From this place, I can partner with God to address the real wound.

It's important to be aware of our own hearts, and of those around us who may be walking through a deeply painful season. It takes wisdom and emotional intelligence to know where our e-motions are taking us. While James encourages us to *"count it all joy"* in the midst of suffering (James 1:2 NKJV), this is not a "fake it 'til we make it" lesson. James is offering hope for a life of beauty arising from these ashes.

We can be thankful for who God is, and for what He is working on in and through our circumstances, while also holding our pain before Him with all of the anger, questions, and fears that come up in the process.

Can a Broken Heart Be Healed?

One of the ways God has revealed Himself in the Bible is by the name Great Physician. I held tightly to this revelation as I walked out my healing. God not only wants to heal every broken body; He longs to heal our broken souls. Our soul is who we are—our mind, will, and emotions. It's how we think and reason, our passions and desires, our choices and feelings.

When my heart was broken, it felt as though the wound was incurable—that I was incurable. But every day I brought my broken heart, broken trust, and self-doubt before God. As I mentioned earlier, I took Communion often, and bringing my broken soul before God was part of this encounter. Every day, He exchanged another piece of my broken soul for a piece of His whole, perfect, and living essence.

How does God work with our heartache and grief? "He heals the brokenhearted and bandages their wounds" (Psalm 147:3).

What is a broken heart? The Hebrew word for *break* or *broken*, *šāḇar*,[1] carries these meanings:

- *to burst*
- *break down*
- *break off*
- *break into pieces*
- *break up*
- *be brokenhearted*
- *bring to birth*
- *crush*
- *destroy*
- *hurt*
- *quench*
- *tear*

Take your time with this list. Which word resonates the most with you? As you think about that, hold gently before the Great Physician every way that you have experienced breaking. And know that God never wants to leave us in our brokenhearted state. His promise is that our broken hearts will be healed, and our wounds will be bound, bandaged, and restrained.

The Hebrew word for heart, *lēḇ*, refers to your feelings, your intellect, your core, and your center or inner being.[2] This is what we refer to as the soul, consisting of your will, conscience, moral character, and the seat of your desires, emotions, passions, and courage. When God says He heals the brokenhearted, He means that our heart, in all of its meanings, can be broken. How you think and choose can be abused and beaten. Your ability for love and connection can be crushed. Your desires, personality, and courage can be broken down to a shadow of what He intended you to be.

Yet every crushed and broken soul can be made completely whole. Where our trust, will, emotions, ambitions, conscience, or courage have been shattered or destroyed, Jesus restrains the sorrow and holds back the hurt. He becomes the healing bandage that aligns and holds all the pieces together. "But [in fact] He has borne our griefs, and He has carried our sorrows and pains…" (Isaiah 53:4 AMP).

Healing as you sort through the aftermath of an affair is messy, hard, and ugly. Months into working to restore our marriage, it didn't seem as though it was going to survive. I thought for sure we were done. I was crushed, but we seemed to just be going in circles. One early morning before I even had a chance to get coffee in my system, Duncan and I got into an argument. Round and round we went. In frustration, I pounded my fist into the arm of the couch. Hard.

It's interesting how we can convince ourselves that we are fine when we are not. It took a week of serious coaxing from a nurse friend before I could be convinced that I should see a doctor. My hand was just as swollen as the day I had punched the couch. Ugly bruising had surfaced, and my hand's movement and use were severely limited. Yet I convinced myself, *It's not that bad.* I had never broken a bone before. But when I do something, I go all out. It required surgery, several screws, and a plate to put the bone between my pinky finger and wrist back in the right place. I joke with Duncan that the metal in my hand costs more than the metal and diamond on my hand. It was an expensive lesson.

After surgery, that wound needed to be *bound*. Movement was restrained while my body poured life and healing into the area. After that, it was time to go to physical therapy to restore movement and function, and to break up the scar tissue. It was painful and took time for the wound to heal, and for freedom to be restored.

During the healing process, we can feel limited and restrained as the pieces are put back together. We will have days in the process that we barely notice or even forget our wounds. Other days, without warning the pain surges through our soul again. Culture has coined a phrase for this experience: *being triggered*. The pain of our broken heart will surge through our soul without notice, leaving us paralyzed, or running.

Like physical healing, God sometimes heals in an instant, and sometimes in a process.

The process of our emotional healing brings connection and trust with God and others. We don't get amnesia about what happened, but we can get to a place where the trauma no longer causes pain. I still have a thin, inch-long scar along the side of my hand where the surgeon cut me open to put me back together.

Your soul may bear the scar of the surgery, but the wound is healed and you are free.

Your soul may bear the scar of the surgery, but the wound is healed and you are free. I remember my final check-in with the hand surgeon. He was happy with the work and the healing. I mountain bike pretty aggressively, and I was concerned about undoing something. *How strong could those tiny screws really be?!* I wondered.

The surgeon assured me that I could not undo his work. Our scar tissue wants to pull us back into fear: *Maybe things are coming undone . . . maybe I'm not really healed.* We need to hear our Surgeon's voice when we are triggered: *You are whole and healed. What you're feeling is just the scar tissue. Let's break it up some more. It's just part of the process.*

We are all working through the effects that sin has had on the image of God in us, and this cannot be ignored. When we ignore the pieces of what makes us human, and the pieces of our humanity that have been broken, we are prone to making terrible decisions and getting stuck.

The worst decisions people make come from a place of avoiding pain, ignoring grief, and generally not dealing with their heart issues. Self-hatred, trauma, fear, loss, shame . . . when we try to escape the negative rather than address it and walk through it with God and friends, we make terrible choices as we try to numb, deny, escape, and ignore our "check engine light."

For yourself or for others going through hell right now, please take these words to heart: Emotions are not bad. Bad emotions are not bad. When we experience them, they're letting us know that there are places inside that still need healing. And when or how we are healed is between us and God.

Don't minimize your process (or someone else's) because the emotions are uncomfortable. You are human, and sometimes life will break you. But God can heal a broken soul. Take your broken mind, thoughts, heart, trust, and love to Him. He is faithful. He is the Healer, the Great Physician, who longs to care for your wounds.

PART THREE

becoming unraveled

to be disengaged or disentangled

to come apart by, or as if by separating the threads of

to have the intricacy, complexity, or obscurity of resolved: to be cleared up[1]

- EIGHTEEN -
Light & Water

As John, a disciple of Jesus, sits down to pen the story of Jesus' time on earth, he begins his gospel with this: "A fountain of life was in him, for his life is light for all humanity. And this Light never fails to shine through darkness—Light that darkness could not overcome!" (John 1:4–5 TPT).

This was Jesus as John knew Him: the Light that broke through every darkness. The Life that redeemed every death.

I pray this is the Jesus that we come to know also.

Psalm 18 has been one of my favorite Scriptures for a long time.[1] I love the poetic imagery of the passionate rescue mission Jesus is on for each one of our hearts.

For when the cords of death wrapped around me
and torrents of destruction overwhelmed me,
taking me to death's door,
in my distress I cried out to you, the delivering God,
and from your temple-throne you heard my troubled cry,
and my sobs went right into your heart. . . .

*Suddenly the brilliance of his presence broke through
with lightning bolts and hail--
A tempest dropping coals of fire. . . .*

He released his lightning-arrows, and routed my foes. . . .

*He rescued me from the mighty waters
and drew me to himself!
Even though I was helpless in the hands
of my hateful, strong enemy,
you were good to deliver me.
When I was at my weakest, my enemies attacked—
but the Lord held on to me.
His love broke open the way,
and he brought me into a beautiful, broad place.*

He rescued me—because his delight is in me! . . .

*God, all at once you turned on a floodlight for me!
You are the revelation-light in my darkness,
And in your brightness I can see the path ahead.
With you as my strength I can crush an enemy horde,
advancing through every stronghold that stands in front of me.*

Or, put more simply in the words of John, *"this Light never fails to shine through darkness—Light that darkness could not overcome"* has come for us.

In despair, I cried out as waves beat and crushed and consumed me. Fear, shame, humiliation, anger, and so much grief were pulling me under. I couldn't breathe; I couldn't see straight. *"Jesus, help"* was all I could whisper.

His strong hand was there, lifting me above the waves. You can call out to Him too. He is near and will not let you go under!

Stepping Out of the Boat

I love the account of Peter, a disciple of Jesus, getting out of a boat, in a storm, to walk on water toward Jesus. A group of men are trying to cross the lake. They are far from land and are in trouble, battling strong winds and heavy waves. The biblical account tells us that it's about 3:00 in the morning when they see a figure walking toward them on the water. These men, who had been raised to fish and had encountered plenty of terrible storms, are afraid.

It's Peter who calls out to the figure on the water:

> Then Peter called to him, "Lord, if it's really you, tell me to come to you, walking on the water."
>
> "Yes, come," Jesus said.
>
> Peter went over the side of the boat and walked on the water toward Jesus. Matthew 14:28-29

Jesus taught that those who follow Him will know His voice. This is the only reason I can think of that Peter would step out of a boat with huge waves crashing in on all sides. Getting out of a boat in a storm is a crazy idea, unless you know and trust the voice of the One calling you.

I am certain that I wouldn't have asked Jesus to call me out onto the water. My response would have been, "Hop in, Jesus, grab an oar, and help us get this thing to shore! We're exhausted!" Nope. Peter stops their progress toward dry land and safety to get out of a boat in the middle of the sea (in a raging storm!), for the opportunity to walk on water. *Hang on, guys, I cannot pass up this opportunity!*

Inside the safety of our "boats," the waves and wind can be brutal. We're wet and cold, struggling to make progress. But we're *in* the boat! It feels safe, even as we dump buckets of water over the side and strain against the oars to get to shore. Are we begging Jesus to "hop in and help," while we're missing the sound of His voice inviting us to walk on water?

If I had taken the risk of trusting my heart sooner, could this storm have been avoided? I was so afraid to rock the boat. I knew my husband wasn't okay, and the longer he wasn't okay, the more I knew we weren't okay. I was too afraid to take the first step to address the disconnection. Eventually, getting out of the boat, as Jesus called me to come closer to Him in the storm, was my only option. Waterlogged, and desperately rowing a sinking boat, I knew it was time to trust.

Can you imagine those massive, crashing waves as we see them from above, from inside our boat? How different, how much more intimidating, are the waves as we are lowered over the side of the boat? Powerfully rolling up and crashing down, these waves are not easily ignored. Peter took a few steps before the waves crashing around him demanded his attention. A fishing career that included a history with storms brought logic front and center: *This is crazy! People outside of boats on the water don't walk—they sink!*

His friend Matthew, likely also in the boat, records the scene for us:

> But when he saw the strong wind and the waves, he was terrified and began to sink. "Save me, Lord!" he shouted.
>
> Jesus immediately reached out and grabbed him. "You have so little faith," Jesus said. "Why did you doubt me?" Matthew 14:30–31

Made to Walk on Water

Confusion comes quickly when we feel as if God has called us to step out of the boat, to move in faith—only we find ourselves sinking. Jesus asks, *Why did you doubt Me?* Keeping our eyes on Jesus is how we overcome when the storms demand our attention. There will be days we sink into anxiety and fear. Gasping for air, crying out to Jesus, we will feel His strong arm pull us to safety again and again. *Do not doubt Me. I am with you in the storm, and you were made to walk on water!*

> **Gasping for air, crying out to Jesus, we will feel His strong arm pull us to safety again and again.**

It was in the storm that I came to know Jesus by His name *Prince of Peace*. The One I look to isn't worried about circumstances. He releases peace into me that doesn't make sense, and He calms my anxious, fearful heart. *Do not doubt me. You can trust that I am good.*

The story of Peter on (and in) the water ends with a statement that we can hold as a promise: "When they climbed back into the boat, the wind stopped" (verse 32). When I was fighting anxious thoughts and battling fear about my future, I spoke a prayer over myself: *I release the peace of Jesus over my heart, my body, and my mind. I am safe, and His strong arm rescues me. I will not go under in this storm.*

I declared that the storms of fear, anxiety, shame, confusion, humiliation, and trauma were to *Be still*. Jesus climbed into the boat with me, and the wind stopped. He will hear your prayers amid the howling wind and storm-tossed waves, too, and will climb in right next to you.

- NINETEEN -
Calming Storms

I find it comforting that Jesus faced betrayal and rejection, death and loss. He was criticized and lied about. He was misunderstood, even by His closest friends. One of His team members betrayed Him for personal gain. Another betrayed Him out of self-protection. Jesus makes an interesting statement to His followers before His surrender to death on the cross: "Here on earth you will have many trials and sorrows. But take heart, because I have overcome the world" (John 16:33).

In Isaiah 43:1–3, the One who can calm any storm tells us this:

> Do not be afraid, for I have ransomed you. I have called you by name; you are mine. When you go through deep waters, I will be with you. When you go through rivers of difficulty, you will not drown. When you walk through the fire of oppression, you will not be burned up; the flames will not consume you. For I am the Lord, your God, Holy One of Israel, your Savior.

What comes to mind when you hear the word *overcoming*? I wonder how many of us think of it as, *If I can just power through this painful event or struggle, then life will be glorious and easy.* We imagine life beyond pain—skipping through puddles and blowing on dandelions, without a care in the world. But that is not what Jesus told us to expect. He said, "Here on earth you will have many trials and sorrows." This is not the promise of a comfortable, pain-free life. The expectation is that we can have peace and find comfort, courage, and even joy, in the middle of the suffering we will experience. This is possible because of the victory He won.

Overcoming is not specifically about any one circumstance. Overcoming is a lifelong posture of keeping our heart's affection and attention on God, no matter how devastating the circumstance. We don't overcome circumstances; we overcome in spite of them. Without connection to love and life, we are fearful and lifeless. But when we hear His heartbeat of love, we access life in the midst of every challenge, pain, or loss. We learn to access peace and joy, no matter what the outcome is. Even when we seemingly go under . . .

You're Not Going Under

The imagery of water in the Bible fascinates me. We find allegorical language to show our lives being pulled up out of the waters. Besides the account of Peter walking on water that we just looked at, we find accounts of the Israelites fleeing from slavery, the Red Sea retreating before them. We see a man named Jonah thrown willingly into the water, where he was swallowed by a great fish that he resided in for three days before being spit up on a beach. We see the practice of water baptism, symbolizing being one with Jesus in His death, burial, and resurrection, rising into a new life.

Water is necessary for life. Water can also destroy life. Rain brings an abundant harvest. A flood destroys the crop. Floating on water brings a sense of calm, so much so that there is now research around the benefits of "float therapy," a practice of spending time floating in sensory-deprivation water tanks to relieve anxiety. Submerge just one foot deeper under the water, however, and our fear rises, heart races, and lungs scream for air.

When circumstances are rising above what we can manage, Jesus promises that we will not go under the waves of the storm. To overcome any storm, we must keep our eyes on Jesus. This does not mean we are delusional about what's raging around us. Overcoming is to be aware of His presence with us in the storm, and simply to do the next right thing. Jesus will pull us out of the deep waters when we sink, and He has even been known to calm storms.

Speak to the Storm

We can tell storms to be still. Spiritual, mental, and emotional hurricanes, and even physical storms, will retreat at our command. We have that authority in Christ. He calmed storms of every kind, and He said we would do greater works than He did (see John 14:12).

Have you ever noticed that sometimes a feeling, struggle, or thought seems to bombard you out of nowhere? Unusual confusion or chaos can begin to press in, tempting you to take your eyes off the peace you've experienced with Jesus. As you talk to friends, you find that they, too, are feeling these same things. That indicates something in the spiritual atmosphere that must be addressed.

I am not one to look for evil in every thought or circumstance I don't like. Nothing makes me more frustrated than Christians calling every difficulty—many caused by their own lack of planning or discipline—"spiritual warfare." Our unhealed thoughts, feelings, and beliefs causing friction and division is not spiritual warfare. Our lack of discipline in our time, health, relationships, or finances is not spiritual warfare.

How do we identify actual spiritual warfare? How do we distinguish between our thoughts and beliefs that we need to address, and an enemy-generated spiritual storm that is trying to get us to believe a lie or partner with death? To know the difference, we need to grow in discernment and wisdom.

The specks of irritation that bother us most about others are often pointing to the deeply rooted tree of an issue in our own heart.

Wisdom in this area begins with learning to recognize what our own heart is struggling with. The first step is to *listen to yourself*. That's it. What are you saying? What complaint do you repeat over and over? In what areas are you most critical of others. If you're not sure, ask a friend. I promise, he or she will know. The specks of irritation that bother us most about others are often pointing to the deeply rooted tree of an issue in our own heart. It's as if our souls know that our character is out of alignment with what is good. So we demand more and better from everyone around us, not realizing that the source of the dissonance is not others, but ourselves.

I've learned to listen to what I say. I've learned to notice the biggest struggles that I have with others. This gives me insight into what issues in my own soul need to be addressed. I ask God what lies I am believing. As He reveals a lie to me, I begin replacing it with His truth. This is an important process as we step out onto the battlefield. We must know our own weaknesses and give them to God.

As I battled for our marriage, I had to face my own soul. I had to be honest about my own fears and weaknesses. I knew that honor and respect were vital to marriage. Yet I didn't grow up seeing those modeled. It wasn't enough to pray for Duncan, or for a healed marriage, if I wasn't also going to address where I myself needed both self-awareness and freedom.

Authority over the Atmosphere

I am from the dry, cool mountain air of Colorado. Last year we flew to Los Angeles, California, for a business conference and family trip. The moment we got off the plane, my girls asked, "Why is the air *sticky*?!"

I remember as a child flying to see family in Louisiana and feeling the same way about the musty, damp air that felt so unfamiliar. Living with *zero* humidity at home, Louisiana seemed like stepping into a swamp. As we learn to discern what's happening in the spiritual realm, it can feel the same way—like walking off a plane into an unfamiliar climate.

Hopefully, most of your spiritual life is marked by a peaceful, loving atmosphere. Hopefully, you spend time with Jesus and experience love, peace, and clarity on a regular basis. When this shifts, however, it can feel as if you've been dropped into an icky, mucky swamp. It's as noticeable as getting on a plane in the dry air of Denver, and stepping off the plane into the humidity of Baton Rouge. When we learn to discern what's in the spiritual atmosphere around us, we have the opportunity to partner with God. We can step into our authority to command spiritual storms to cease, so that we, and others, can row the boats we're in safely to the shore.

Practically, what I mean when I say "I sense" or "I feel" these things in the atmosphere is that a sudden thought or feeling will come to me. Thoughts of a bad accident, hopelessness, or death suddenly enter my thoughts, bringing all kinds of bad feelings and images with them. I've learned that such thoughts are not my own, but are coming at me from the enemy to take me, my family, or my community down.

When I sense this type of shift in an atmosphere, I begin to declare that the fear and lies saturating the air, so to speak, have no power in that place or the people, including me. Then I release God's life, the antidote, the truth, His Word. When confusion is swirling, I command it to be still, followed by asking God to release clarity and peace. Or when I feel a heavy spirit of death, I can hear and feel suicidal thoughts as if they were my own. I have learned to resist this spirit and speak to this kind of storm, commanding the swirling winds and waves to cease. I ask the Holy Spirit to release life and hope and peace into the atmosphere instead.

As followers of Jesus, we have the authority to calm the storms that threaten us and threaten others. There are dark strategies laid out against us that we must understand and stand against. When we are suffering, we are susceptible to being overcome by darkness.

When in pain, we need to be aware of the atmospheres we allow and create. Anger, fear, and unforgiveness invite evil to swirl and rage around us. Learning to choose love and walk in forgiveness is our greatest weapon against these forces. The more we learn to walk in the reality of God's love, the better we get at it, and the more victory in peace we experience.

As I healed, I experienced days when I felt defeated, broken, and completely unable to walk in love or forgiveness. But I knew God's love. So I got up again and again to keep trying. I faced off with dark thoughts and overwhelming fears. Slowly, bit by bit, I overcame, and the storm sent to destroy me turned into a gentle rain of refreshing. I was not going to go under. You don't have to go under either.

- TWENTY -
Moving Mountains

On the heels of painful events or seasons of waiting for breakthrough, there are temptations that await us. We can survive the storm, yet wind up stuck in the wreckage on the shore. The goal of temptation is to cause us to doubt God's goodness and love, and to lure us into activities that we can manage and control (or so we think).

Temptation comes knocking when we are tired of fighting the battles and just want the pain to stop. Temptation convinces us that there is a shortcut. When we can't see a way forward, temptation whispers in the dark, *Look how good this little pleasure over here looks. You can take hold of this habit and feel so much better. You are under so much pressure . . . you deserve this. It will only be this once. You need this. No one really understands you. You've got to do it your own way. You have a right to enjoy life, too!*

The danger of temptation is not in what we do, or don't do. The real destruction is that we doubt God's goodness, turning toward self to fulfill our needs and desires. Desire lures us into coping, soothing, and medicating away pain, at the cost of real love and transformation.

Taking the bait, we rationalize small lies. Harbor little lusts. Cover up a growing addiction to substances, sex, or entertainment. Justify being unkind and manipulative. Compromising a little here, a little there. We drift slowly from life into death one dopamine hit at a time, calling it freedom.

We All Want to Feel Better

Why am I telling you all of this? You're not the one whose choices set off a path of destruction. You're reading this book to get through the pain someone else caused you—to feel better, not to learn about temptations and sin.

I tell you all of this because we all want to feel better. To feel wholly, fully, joyfully alive. After a painful event, unmet desires will come knocking at our door. We're given an opportunity to turn toward self to meet those needs, just as those who hurt us have done. It's time to stop the cycle of false comfort and instant gratification.

We cannot afford to be blind to the enemy's schemes and strategies set on destroying our faith and our relationships. Whatever situation you found yourself in was only the beginning of what you must walk through. I know you can get through this really, truly whole and free. I did.

There were so many times I cried out to God, *Will I ever be okay?* I felt so messed up, so damaged, so afraid of everyone and everything. Broken and sad. It just didn't seem possible to love and trust and be happy again. But God is truly good, and faithful to walk through it all with us.

What is it that leaves us shipwrecked? Unbelief. The lie that whispers, *God is not really good. He does not really love you. He cannot be trusted.* Maybe you've heard it articulated this way: *God caused and allowed this destruction in order to teach you a lesson.*

Painful events cause us to doubt that God can be trusted. So we question, *Does He really love me? Does He want the best for me?* Doubting God's goodness shifts our focus to finding ways to protect ourselves, provide for ourselves, and trust only ourselves.

> ***If waters are the circumstances we must walk through, mountains are the temptations we face when we get to the shore.***

If waters are the circumstances we must walk through, mountains are the temptations we face when we get to the shore. The traumatic event is over and in the past. We made it through. Now, however, we have work to do: We have to overcome unbelief.

The Strategies of Unbelief

You can spot the strategies of unbelief a mile away if you know this: *You have an enemy who wants to lure you away from God by convincing you that He is not good.* This is the lie Adam and Eve were presented with in the new and beautiful world, the place where they experienced unbroken fellowship with God:

> The serpent was the shrewdest of all the wild animals the Lord God had made. One day he asked the woman, "Did God really say you must not eat the fruit from any of the trees in the garden?"
>
> "Of course we may eat fruit from the trees in the garden," the woman replied. "It's only the fruit from the tree in the middle of the garden that we are not allowed to eat. God said, 'You must not eat it or even touch it; if you do, you will die.'"
>
> "You won't die!" the serpent replied to the woman. "God knows that your eyes will be opened as soon as you eat it, and you will be like God, knowing both good and evil." Genesis 3:1-5

The result of this exchange came in the form of a question that arose in Eve's mind: *Maybe God is withholding something good from us?*

This is the same temptation Jesus overcame in the wilderness: *If you are the Son of God . . . you should not be experiencing this humble, sacrificial existence.* The devil's words were meant to make Jesus question His Father's motives and affection. The core of such questions causes us to doubt God's goodness. So we ask ourselves, *Does God really care about you? Here you are, in the middle of nowhere, hungry, hot, and tired. Has He abandoned you?* And we are tempted to meet our own needs, in case He will not. It can be terrifying to entrust our hearts to God in the aftermath of betrayal. It is these doubts and fears about His nature that make it so difficult. Doubts and fears are natural and must be faced in order to move forward. If we believe temptations and pain are God's plan for our training, we are left wondering if His "teaching" can be endured.

James warns us never to say "God is tempting me," because, as he goes on to say, "God is never tempted to do wrong, and he never tempts anyone else" (James 1:13). God will never use temptation to "teach you a lesson," as many have claimed. Giving in to temptation is rooted in *unbelief* and results in covering, fulfilling, and justifying our needs in our own power. The rest of James's message here explains,

> Temptation comes from our own desires, which entice us and drag us away. These desires give birth to sinful actions. And when sin is allowed to grow, it gives birth to death. So don't be misled, my dear brothers and sisters. Whatever is good and perfect is a gift coming down to us from God our Father, who created all the lights in the heavens. He never changes or casts a shifting shadow. He chose to give birth to us by giving us his true word. And we, out of all creation, became his prized possession. James 1:14–18

James explains that temptations come to nudge our trust away from God and lure us into fulfilling our legitimate needs in illegitimate ways. *Our own desires entice us and drag us away.* We all have legitimate needs and desires. To name a few, we all long for and need affection, attention, love, community, purpose, and fulfillment. When we don't trust God in the process, we will meet our desires and needs in our own timing, in our own way, and by our own hands. Has this led us to believe that the problem is with our desires rather than with misplaced trust?

God will never employ evil to teach, train, or grow us. It is our own desires that entice us. Not brought before God, these desires rage within us, demanding that we *overcome pain by any means.* So we drown our desires in alcohol, food, entertainment, or sex.

Meeting our legitimate needs for pleasure, connection, peace, meaning, and sustenance in illegitimate ways, we will cause more damage to our bodies and souls than any storm we will face. We think the mountain of temptation for self-gratification will rescue us from the waves, and lift us out of the pain, to higher ground. Only to discover that we are ensnared in more pain and more death, and are merely numbed and disconnected from life, meaning, and relationships.

Our Powerful Weapons

God teaches, trains, and equips sons and daughters through His Word, not through temptations or trials. His ever-speaking Word is a powerful enough weapon to help us cut through the chatter of the wind, and remove mountains. Enabling us to discern clearly the lies of self. Giving us grace to trust that God really did say He is good, and has good plans for us.

It's time to rewrite the story. Others have stayed shipwrecked, angry, and bitter, continuing a cycle of pain—attempting to protect themselves and feel better in ways that invite more darkness. If we do not face head on both the storm and the mountains, we will remain stuck in the past, repeating the painful and broken circumstances in new ways to those around us.

That's not our legacy. We can stop the patterns of destruction. We can stand against demonic strategies by refusing to loosen our grip on two of the most powerful weapons we have: *forgiveness* and *love*.

- TWENTY-ONE -
ROAD CLOSED

Whoa there, you might be thinking, *this book just got super weird*. Friend, the battle for your heart is real, and I cannot leave you without the insight and tools I've learned to employ in overcoming relational trauma and the battles I experienced in the aftermath.

One simple thing I did was to declare *ROAD CLOSED* to the thoughts that tried to derail me. This was a daily, even hourly practice until the roads leading to the negative, accusatory, angry thoughts were no longer accessible.

It was through reading Mike Hutchings's book *Supernatural Freedom from the Captivity of Trauma* that I learned to say *ROAD CLOSED* to the traumatic thoughts and movies that played on repeat night and day in my soul.

Imagine your brain's neural pathways as roads for the vehicles carrying your thoughts around. Some paths are ruts, narrow and deep. The ruts get deeper each time you give attention to a specific thought. This is a gift as we learn to play an instrument or memorize beautiful poetry. However, this God-given design can also entrench negative thought patterns unless we actively notice and address them.

We also have less-used thought pathways. The thoughts on these pathways are fading and becoming obsolete. My fifth-grade English teacher and the rules of various childhood games are long-lost thoughts. These pathways were never utilized after the information was no longer useful. Other pathways have become superhighways. These roads can feel inescapable, with thoughts going at lightning speed, multiple on-ramps, and too much traffic. The depth and frequency of these thought patterns can be elevated by our pain.

When I felt triggered by all the pain, I would say out loud *ROAD CLOSED* to shake the bombardment of negativity off my thoughts. I imagined myself putting up orange-and-white traffic barricades with flashing lights and *ROAD CLOSED* written across them in bold letters. This imagery, and speaking aloud, helped me stop the thoughts, accusations, and assumptions from going any further.

A valuable lesson I learned from Hutchings was that these painful memories do not need to torment me. Through practicing what he teaches, I can now remember and discuss this painful season without mental torment.

Here's what I would do in difficult moments: When my attention was drawn to the flashbacks and negative thoughts, I imagined the road barricaded, I declared (out loud, as often as it was appropriate) *ROAD CLOSED*, and I prayed,

> *In Jesus' name, I declare this road closed and no longer available for meditation. In Jesus' name, every harmful, traumatic memory may no longer torment me. Though I won't forget what has happened, these memories are not allowed to cause me pain!*

I learned that I could heal my physical brain, and even rewire it. This helped me heal. We do not have to partner with the torment of painful memories. We can stop the tormenting thoughts and be free to heal! For the longest time, anything and everything that reminded me of what had happened would send me into pure rage. I'll spare you the details. But I will tell you this: Those same triggers, even names and places, no longer cause me torment of any kind. There is true freedom available!

Canceling Unholy, Unhealthy Agreements

I also learned in my healing process about agreements. We all make them, and they're not always good. We have often made unholy, unhealthy agreements with harmful thought patterns or even evil spirits without realizing it.

I struggled with fantasizing about finding a new marriage partner and leaving behind all this baggage. It was alluring to play the movies in my mind of what a new life and partner could be like. This was a spirit of fantasy wanting me to partner with impossibly perfect outcomes and abort the progress Duncan and I were making at reconciliation. Fantasy lures us out of reality, hope, and healthy relationships. Don't confuse fantasy with God-inspired imagination, which releases hope.

The most aggressive agreement I wanted to make was with *accusations*. Call it a spirit or a demon. Call it an agreement. Call it pure evil, but accusations were the most pernicious thought patterns I had to break.

The devil is called *the accuser of the brethren* (see Revelation 12:10). You can be sure that wherever accusations against someone's character or motives are active, darkness is nearby. I would be going about my day, feeling as though I was making progress, when the most evil and dark thoughts toward others would rise up inside of me. I could feel the poison taking root as I allowed these thoughts, and at times even spoke out the pure evil.

Then I would remember, *ROAD CLOSED*.

I learned from *Overcoming Fear* by Dawna De Silva to recognize when I was partnering with an evil spirit, thought, or agreement. I would then acknowledge it, and repent for partnering with it. Next, I listened to the Holy Spirit's whisper. An image, thought, or word would rise up within me containing a truth that expelled the lies. Love replaced fear. Trust and hope could take root a bit more in my heart. My declaration and prayer in those moments went something like this:

> *I see you, spirit of accusation, and I refuse to partner with you. Be gone, in Jesus' name!*
>
> *Jesus, forgive me for allowing accusing, negative, evil thoughts toward this person into my heart. Holy Spirit, thank you for freedom from this fear. I release this person to you.*

From there, I would begin to pray for the person. Accusation is assigning motives to someone's actions. I can see someone's actions without assigning motives or judgements to the person.

Other versions of accusation are suspicion and assumption. Wounded people call these discernment, but I have found both to be in partnership with accusation. When we've been hurt, we need clarity. Discernment comes from love, not fearful suspicion that assigns motives and leads to punishing others and protecting self.

An agreement that was trickier for me to discern was with *a spirit of rejection*, because I had a long-time partnership with this one. In May of 2019, I remember having a really difficult conversation with Duncan. He was already cold and distant, and he communicated that we were not good for each other and shouldn't be together.

I was shocked. I felt deep rejection. It was then, before I even had the tools I'm sharing with you now, that I decided *I am unrejectable*.

This thought, this idea was truly a gift whispered into my heart. And it was the foundation for the choices and attitudes I made in the years following.

As I learned more, I began to see how I had been in agreement with rejection and abandonment for most of my life. Now, I could cancel this contract and replace it with knowing the love of Father God, who had chosen me and loved me before the creation of the world.

Today when I feel rejection swirling, I look to my heart to be sure I'm not partnering with this damaging spirit in some way. I get quiet with Jesus, lay this before Him, and ask some questions. If I need to, I repent for partnering with rejection, and I ask the Holy Spirit to fill me again with God's love.

Dealing with a Spirit of Death

Another darkness that tried to attach to me during this season was of depression and death. I was brokenhearted, and struggling deeply. At some point, a spirit of death felt as if it were overcoming me. I am not sure how far into our reconciliation we were at this point. I only remember that Duncan had taken the girls out for a bit, and I suddenly became overwhelmed with images of hanging myself in the bathroom.

It wasn't about grief, or getting out of the way, or feeling as if I couldn't go on. But it was a powerful force trying to get me to agree with a spirit of death. This was one of those times when I could only pray, *Jesus, help.*

I repeated that prayer until I could declare more, similar to the earlier prayer I shared. I would call out what was trying to overtake me, command it to go in Jesus name, and declare life and peace and the blood of Jesus over myself spirit, soul, and body.

Hear me on this: I haven't struggled with depression or suicide ever before. I learned a long time ago that at times I would sense these spirits in the atmosphere around me, and I would then pray for the people nearby. I have only felt a spirit of death so forcefully one other time since that day. We all need to learn what is ours, and what we are sensing around us. With that said, if you are struggling, please ask for help. I remember telling Duncan later that night what I had experienced. I truly believe this was a key to being free from the hold death was trying to take on me. Confession is powerful. It brings things trying to grow in darkness into the light, where freedom is.

> *Confession is powerful. It brings things trying to grow in darkness into the light, where freedom is.*

Comparison seems more subtle, but still could have taken me under, if I had made an agreement with it. It would have been easy to keep dwelling on questions like *Why wasn't I good enough? What was I lacking? How can I be sexier and more fun?* The truth is, affairs don't happen because the spouse is lacking anything, but rather because the person being unfaithful is trying to fill a void in himself or herself. Prayer, journaling, and letting God speak life into my identity were keys to freedom from this agreement. God's love is perfect and whole and removes our fear. Even the fear of not being enough. Isn't that what comparison is?

A Key That Released Breakthrough

This chapter's list of unholy and unhealthy agreements isn't comprehensive, but I hope it gives you the tools needed to recognize and address the attacks coming against your freedom and healing. As I learned to do this over myself, I also began to ask God for the key to the agreements, lies, and attacks that Duncan was facing.

What God revealed to me was the key that opened the door to Duncan's freedom, and closed the door once and for all to his previous choices. For months, I prayed and struggled to pin down exactly what lie he was believing. I prayed generically that God would help him overcome any lies he was believing about himself, about me, about our marriage. Finally I heard one word, the key that unlocked our healing: *seduction.*

Seduction tells us that we are missing out on something—that the next best thing is out there and we don't have it. This spirit keeps us from taking hold of what is good today, as we search for something else to fill us. It also keeps us from the One and Only who can make us whole—Jesus.

This wasn't the only prayer or warfare I did for Duncan or our marriage. But this was the one that seemed to release the breakthrough for us. As with the other unholy agreements I found lurking, I prayed for freedom from this lie and agreement.

Discernment Draws the Line

What lies, agreements, or attacks do you need to stand against today so that you can walk in all the freedom God has for you?

If we are to walk free and whole, we must develop discernment. Not suspicion. Not assumptions. Not devil-focused, weirdo pseudo-spirituality. Ask God to give you insight and wisdom into what's going on in the spiritual realm. This just means that you know what's going on spiritually around you and are aware of what's not in line with God's love.

Developing this kind of discernment will allow you to draw the line between what is a personal habit or mindset issue that's causing you pain, and what is spiritual warfare. When you recognize that you or others are partnering with an evil spirit, thought, or agreement, it can then be acknowledged and disarmed. You can repent for agreeing with any of those, command them to go, and find your freedom in Christ.

And don't forget to tell them *ROAD CLOSED*.

- TWENTY-TWO -
Coffee Cups

When Duncan first revealed his infidelity to me, he opted right away to sleep on the couch in our small home. After two nights, I asked him to move out. I needed space to think, to breathe, to do whatever I wanted or needed without him there. I don't know how to explain it, but I needed to feel safe in my own space. Duncan has never and would never physically hurt me or the girls. He is not an emotionally or mentally abusive person. Yet *safety* was the word that came to mind. I needed to be able to react to this pain without worrying about his reaction. I needed space to pace, worship, and cry. Get up a million times for a glass of water. Without anyone knowing.

When I first asked this of him, I thought it would be two weeks, tops. This would give me time to sort out all my thoughts and emotions before we started working toward living in the same space again. There were emotional and practical things to figure out, and I knew I couldn't and shouldn't try to make all of these decisions immediately. I knew I didn't have to decide today if we would stay together or not. I just needed to decide what was best for "today." What did I need to feel safe and move one step forward in the best way possible now, not forever?

Asking Duncan to leave was a huge risk. Would he be gone forever? Was

I providing the perfect opportunity for him to walk away from me and into another relationship?

Giving the Girls a Sense of "Normal"

The girls were "homeschooled" during this time, and I use that term ever so lightly. Their school did not resume after spring break because of the Covid lockdowns. The teachers did their best to provide live video check-ins with their class and assigned fun, but probably not ideal educational material for parents to administer.

I did my best, carrying the weight of it on top of everything else. But it did provide the girls with my focused time and attention for a few hours each day, at a time when it felt hard to focus on anything. In that sense, the "homeschooling" provided beautiful and connected moments for the girls and me.

Duncan would come home around noon each day, after the girls' schoolwork was finished. We would spend the day as "normally" as possible, considering all of the things that were happening. I would have time to work and get out of the house. We would do dinner, baths, and bedtime as a family.

After the girls were tucked in, Duncan and I would check in with each other. There were great conversations and really hard conversations. Sometimes, I just wanted to rage at him. Remind him how stupid he had been. (And to be honest, there were times when I did this, and it was awful.) I also knew it was going to take great self-control on my part to demonstrate the forgiveness I had given. I did my best to stay curious and open. I was also determined to have real conversations, including addressing the lies Duncan was believing. Some nights, our check-ins were a short 20 minutes. Other times, they were much longer.

By the time their dad left for the apartment he had rented, both girls should have been asleep. Our youngest daughter, just three years old, fell asleep quickly each night. Our nine-year-old, who has never been interested in missing out on life just to sleep, would call to me as soon as Duncan's car pulled away. Her room window had a view of the driveway. She would watch him leave, and then call for me. I would go and lie in bed with her for as long as I could hold myself together, trying to comfort her while processing my conversation minutes earlier with Duncan in my head—and being heartbroken that it was another night Duncan and I were not ready to be in the same home.

We told the girls that Dad had a big work project to figure out, and that's why he wasn't there when they woke up in the mornings. I'm not sure they believed it. They could feel that something was off.

We did our best to make sure the girls felt loved and safe during this time. Yet we never outright told them what was going on. We would reassure them during difficult days that we were working through something really hard, but that it was not their fault, or their problem to solve. To this day, my heart breaks at the pain I know they absorbed, that we all absorbed, during this time.

Two Coffee Cups

After several weeks, I came to the point where I wasn't a complete mess after Duncan left. Each night before I closed the house down and went to bed, I would get the coffee ready for the next morning. I also set out two coffee cups. Mine, and Duncan's.

Though I would never have said it out loud at the time, I thought it would be nice for him to have his coffee cup in the morning . . . just in case he decided it was time to come home in the middle of the night.

I thought it would be nice for him to have his coffee cup in the morning ... just in case he decided it was time to come home in the middle of the night.

I wanted Duncan home. He wasn't ready. He was really trying to determine what to do. Either choice had its own ramifications. He was not taking the situation lightly. I understood his hesitation. And it was agonizing.

When I woke up in the morning, I would slip his mug back into the cabinet so no one would know, especially Duncan. It felt so silly to set out two coffee cups each night, but it also felt prophetic, making space for the hope that we would be in the same house again one day.

Other than a few close friends and counselors, we didn't bring many people into our journey. I may be the only person on the planet who was grateful for the Covid lockdowns. Most people were unaware of what we were going through, since they were wrapped up in their own world during that time. No one was hosting gatherings or asking us to hang out. As the world marched to a slower pace, Duncan and I were able to process, talk, and spend time with our girls as a family. This helped us truly heal and move forward.

What I thought would be a couple of weeks turned into just over two months. It's all a blur now. Duncan took that time to decide he was all in on "us" and wanted to heal together. As hope for a healthy marriage settled in his heart and mind, he came home.

The first time we were intimate again, I cried. I knew how powerful and important it was for the two of us to reconnect. I wanted to, but there were so many emotions and thoughts to overcome. While I was the first to initiate intimacy, I also struggled with insecurity and shame. Duncan was so gentle and understanding with my heart during this process. It took a long time to be really, truly free with him again.

I struggle to give you any specific instructions or detailed examples about how I processed this area of our marriage. The truth is, I sometimes feel as if I did it all wrong. Is there really a "right" way to handle any of this? All I can advise is that you take it one step at a time and do what is healthy for you and your spouse.

Each couple, each marriage, each circumstance—they are all so different. Don't look for a pattern to follow; look for principles to live by. Take the steps that lead you to wholeness and healing, whether that ends up being together, or apart. By God's grace and guidance, Duncan and I walked through this season together. Today, I feel more free and safer with him than I ever have.

To this day, we still set out our coffee cups by the coffeemaker each night. And I smile and thank God for the fullness He has brought to us. Duncan's move back into our home did not bring about instant healing, of course. We had come so far, but we had so much more to overcome.

- TWENTY-THREE -
Fire Forged

I have experienced two kinds of fire: the fire of trials, and the fire of God's presence.

Have you ever seen someone who lives so vulnerably, so wholly and powerfully, only to find out later the incredible pain he or she has overcome? People who have overcome the flames of trials carry themselves differently. They live from a deeper place of strength and wisdom. They lead, parent, love, and create powerfully. They have walked through the cruel flames of suffering, allowing everything but Jesus to be burned away.

Those who have met Jesus in the fire of trials manifest tenderness and boldness, marking everyone they meet. A healed heart understands that it was because of the brokenness, not in spite of it, that Jesus was revealed. Those who have overcome live with a love and resolve that few are willing to attain. They illuminate the world around them unashamedly with the light revealed to them in the flames. And they bring this gift purely, wholly, and unshackled. This is how I want to live. This is how I want to love.

The fire of trials and suffering reveals the burdens we carry. These flames will also uncover what our hope and trust are rooted in. What we once thought was necessary, the flames reveal as hindrances. As fear, self-protection, and small thinking are burned away, we must no longer allow their weight to limit us.

The fire of God's presence will burn away the impurities of unbelief that threaten to destroy us and keep us from His goodness. This holy fire is experienced in intimate communion with Him. God's love can heal, reveal, and comfort. He can unravel every wound and lie that keep us bound.

The Fire of Trials

Paul, Peter, and James all teach, as Jesus did, that life will be unbearable at times. It's not a matter of *if* life is painful, but *when*. Not only are trials part of the believer's experience, but Jesus and His disciples communicated that these painful, life-shattering events invite God to do incredible good!

An often-quoted verse used in difficult times is Romans 8:28: "And we know that God causes everything to work together for the good of those who love God and are called according to his purpose for them." The word *everything* in this verse is the Greek word *synergeō*.[1] This is the word we get *synergy* from. God longs to be invited into *everything* in our lives, add Himself to the equation, and weave together an outcome where all the suffering, joy, pain, fun, successes, and failures synergize—empowering the outcome He had in mind for each of us from the beginning: to be like Jesus.

Peter explains trials as a fire that refines and purifies precious metals. Trials can refine our faith. The enemy wants to use these trials to kill, steal, and destroy. To bind and to limit. And ultimately, to extinguish our trust in God. Yet God meets us in the fire to ensure that our faith becomes pure and unmixed. Trials are not from God, yet He will absolutely meet us in the furnace to make sure we have a chance to grow, heal, and overcome. Peter tells us,

> So be truly glad. There is wonderful joy ahead, even though you must

endure many trials for a little while. These trials will show that your faith is genuine. It is being tested as fire tests and purifies gold—though your faith is far more precious than mere gold. So when your faith remains strong through many trials, it will bring you much praise and glory and honor on the day when Jesus Christ is revealed to the whole world. 1 Peter 1:6–7

The refining process of precious metals does not create gold or silver; it removes the impurities. While there are processes that add materials to metal to make it stronger, this is not the goal when refining our faith. God is jealous for our hearts. He is uninterested in sharing our affections with disordered desires rooted in self. He longs for tender and malleable hearts.

Fire needs fuel. The trials meant to consume hope, joy, and love are transformed by God to refine us. We are positioned in a trial to become more Christlike as the flames destroy our disordered desires. When life throws death, betrayal, broken dreams, failed relationships, a hopeless diagnosis, or any other of a myriad of trials at us, we have the opportunity to dig in and find our faith.

In the fire, we have the choice to respond in trust toward God, or to rely on our own power to overcome. Jesus wouldn't give us the promise and command to overcome without giving us the ability. When we feel as if our faith is not enough, could it be that we have buried it so far beneath wrong motives, self-protection, shame, or fear that we have to dig incredibly deep to find this gift from God?

Faith isn't something that we muster up or figure out. Faith is a gift that focuses our attention and trust on who Jesus is, and on what He said is true. Faith is present when we say *yes* to what we believe God is asking of us. Each trial that we face is a chance to see God's goodness and discover that He is faithful to do what He said He would. To remind our hearts that the One we placed our trust in is faithful.

Many say faith is like a muscle that must be given a good workout. I think faith is a gift. As God's children and followers of Christ, we have faith. We are always learning to awaken this gift. We can apply our will, our choosing, and our trusting over and over again, until we are fully convinced that God will come through and be faithful to His Word.

Holding onto what you know to be true about God will carry you through any trial and help you land safely on a new shore with more confidence in Him.

Faith in the Crucible

The language of *testing* in the Bible carries with it the imagery of *a furnace for smelting*. The trials we go through are a crucible. A crucible is a vessel for refining ore and precious metals to extract the impurities. While the tests and trials of life are not fair or good, God in His goodness uses them to approve our faith. *Approving* our faith is not God checking in to see if we can pass this test. Proven faith is faith that has been in the fire of trials and hasn't let go of trust in God. God doesn't need to know where our faith is at. I'm pretty sure He is very clear on that. We're the ones who need to know that faith in God is enough.

When we put the full weight of our trust in Christ and what He said, we discover that He is good and true to His Word. Testing our faith isn't to show God what He has placed inside us, but to open our eyes to the strength of this gift. As we see this about our faith, we will wield it more purposefully, and with more authority, to take down the giants in the land.

> *Testing our faith isn't to show God what He has placed inside us, but to open our eyes to the strength of this gift.*

Before Duncan's actions were revealed, God spoke to me clearly these words from the book of Numbers: *I am not a man, that I should lie.*[2] He imprinted in my heart the reminder that He is who He says He is, does what He says He will do, and will not fail me. These words helped me hold onto what mattered most in this storm—my faith in God.

Within the crucible of a trial, faith meets real life and the heat is on. Here we find impurities, things we trust more than God, be it our income, talents, relationships, doctrine, disciplines, or health. These can become idols that we trust more than God. These are all the things we pile *on top of* our faith, and call it faith.

Jesus says, "If you are faithful in little things, you will be faithful in large ones. But if you are dishonest in little things, you won't be honest with greater responsibilities" (Luke 16:10). I've been taught that this verse means if I do a good job with the little jobs I've been given, I will get better jobs. Yet it can mean so much more. When trials come, we get to practice with the "small trials," although nothing seems small at the time. Will we keep our trust in God and do what we know is right? Or, will we partner with lies and make agreements with our idols to protect ourselves in a moment of pain and pressure?

James explains that when we are in these intense seasons of life, we can rejoice, because the things we had attached to our faith, which are *not* faith in God, will be burned away.

As we encounter Jesus in the flames and allow ungodly trust and attachments to be burned away, James says our patience and endurance will also grow: "When troubles of any kind come your way, consider it an opportunity for great joy. For you know that when your faith is tested, your endurance has a chance to grow" (James 1:2–3). The definition of *patience* or *endurance* in this Scripture is "the characteristic of a man who is not swerved from his deliberate purpose and his loyalty to faith and piety by even the greatest trials and sufferings."[3] James also says, "So let it grow, for when your endurance is fully developed, you will be perfect and complete, needing nothing" (James 1:4).

In this process, two things can happen: We can hold on with all of our strength to the impurities of self-protection, self-justification, and self-fulfillment. Or, we can allow those things to be nailed to the cross with Jesus. Instead of forsaking faith, our ability to face difficulties with complete trust in God increases.

Unbound and Unburned

In Daniel chapter 3, the Bible tells the story of three Hebrew boys thrown into the furnace of an angry, narcissistic king because they would not worship him. The king set up a monument to himself that was ninety feet tall and decided that everyone in his kingdom should bow down in honor and reverence of his greatness. Three Hebrew slaves refused to worship the king's statue.

It looked as though it was going to cost these three slaves their lives to remain loyal to God. These young men were confident that God *could* save them from the flames. They also knew they had to face the flames rather than bow to another, even if God did not show up in the way they hoped. Their speech to the king was an incredibly inspiring testimony of their faith and dedication to God:

> If we are thrown into the blazing furnace, the God whom we serve is able to save us. He will rescue us from your power, Your Majesty. But even if he doesn't, we want to make it clear to you, Your Majesty, that we will never serve your gods or worship the gold statue you have set up. Daniel 3:17–18

Their incredible display of faith in God alone enraged the king and incited him to turn up the heat seven times hotter than normal. The fire was notched up to its full capacity to get those guys to back down, so they would deny their God and their faith in Him by bowing down to this counterfeit deity. The flames were so hot that the soldiers tasked with throwing these three Hebrews into the oven died carrying out their orders.

Can we be real for a minute? How many times have you seen someone going through an intense trial and thought something judgmental? Like, *He must not be honoring God!* Or, *There must be secret sin in her life for her to be experiencing so much hardship!*

It is true that our own choices and thoughts have consequences. Sometimes painfully negative ones. It can also be true that when we give our wholehearted *yes* to God, the evil one we refuse to worship becomes provoked, turning up the furnace to its full capacity. The enemy sees how powerful our faith is, and is terrified.

Three men were forced into the fire, yet four men were seen walking around, seemingly unaffected by the consuming flames around them. "And the fourth looks like a god!" the astonished king shouted (Daniel 3:25). The three young men had to be summoned out of the furnace. The flames had burned away their bondages, yet they had stayed in the fire! They were in no rush to leave, because another Man was in there with them.

If only we had a record of His conversation with them!

The king got as close as he could to the furnace without being burned alive, and shouted at the men to come out. Daniel 3:27 records that "the fire had not touched them. Not a hair on their heads was singed, and their clothing was not scorched. They didn't even smell of smoke!"

They didn't even smell like smoke.

I use this story and its imagery to help us view our darkest moments of life from God's perspective. Maybe we don't go through trials because we failed, but because we were growing, or were standing up for something important. Maybe life is just hard. Maybe people can just be dumb.

No matter the what, why, or how, *when trials come, know that joy will* come, and you will walk out of the flames with faith that is battle-tested and ready for anything.

You don't have to come out smelling like smoke. What was meant to harm can refine. Beware, many fall prey to the temptations of self and come out bitter and brittle instead of tender and refined. I have seen people go through trials and smell like smoke for the rest of their lives. No amount of going to church, Christian conferences, or prayer meetings has washed them of the residue of their pain. They got stuck.

We are all at risk of living each day stuck in a moment of pain, missing the freedom of walking out of the flames unbound and unburned, with a deeper connection to Jesus. We can choose to declare how God has healed, delivered, and set us free. Or we can continue to talk about how unjust it was that we were in the fire in the first place. When we come out of the fire hard, unteachable, cynical, and bitter, we smell like smoke.

Don't get stuck in circumstances and miss encountering the One who showed up with you in the crucible. Of course what happened to you was unjust and unfair. But I don't want you to remain stuck in that moment any longer. You will miss out on so much beauty in this life.

You can be free and whole.

Faith Rises to Face the Giant

David, a young shepherd boy from the Bible, went head-to-head with an enemy king. Goliath was a giant *over nine feet tall*. Being from the Colorado West, I can't help but imagine a high-noon cowboy duel—a young kid with not much more than a zeal for justice and a small pistol, challenging an experienced, sun-weathered outlaw and his posse.

David's response? *With God's help, I've killed a lion and a bear; why not a giant?* (You can read the whole story in 1 Samuel 17). He too, had experience, but his training had been in proving the faithfulness of God. When predators had come against the sheep under David's care, he acted to protect the sheep. Now, a larger enemy was coming against another flock, the people of God, and David already knew God's heart and provision for the situation.

This is the imagery that God showed me as I doubted my ability to truly forgive my husband for his choices. I had forgiven others before this: family members, friends, and leaders had all been a training ground for this moment. The wounds others had inflicted and the trust I had employed to forgive now seemed like such a small feat compared to what was in front of me. But I trusted that with God's help, I could take down this intimidating giant of wounds. I was just a kid with a couple of stones, facing down a giant of unforgiveness.

Faith rises like that. I had forgiven a big prideful cat and an angry bear, metaphorically speaking. I had confidence that this giant of betrayal would also be forgiven, and its power over me would fall. God was with me then; He is with me now.

Whom Are We Fighting?

There is a dark and malignant enemy at work against you, against everyone. His only goal is to destroy your faith in God and God's goodness. Your enemy is not those who have caused you harm, but the temptation to mistrust God.

When we turn away from God, we turn to all kinds of delusions and darkness. Sitting in a church each week does not exempt us from this temptation. While quoting Scriptures, singing in worship, and serving the congregation, we can still allow unbelief to cast shadows in our hearts.

It is important to begin changing our perspective. To begin declaring redemption over our deep wounds, over the circumstances that we didn't ask for, and reminding ourselves of the deep darkness people are enslaved to that would make them capable of what they have done. And to humbly admit that we are also capable of partnering with darkness in our suffering.

David cut the head off the enemy who was mocking God's people and threatening to make them slaves. We must also rise up, trusting that the God who got us through every battle this far will get us through the battle today. With His help, we will unravel every lie. We will not become slaves to what taunts us.

- TWENTY-FOUR -
The *F* Word: Forgiveness

I was often tempted to talk to anyone and everyone about what had happened to me. Getting others to agree that justice needed to be served seemed as if it would make the pain go away. Wouldn't having others tilt their head with empathy and agreement soothe the pain? Someone to say, "Oh yes, that's terrible!"

But I knew, deep down, that any verdict in my favor, on my terms, would be revenge, not justice. Revenge would not make me feel better, would not bring about the healing my heart or marriage needed.

When Duncan proposed to me, I was a flurry of emotions. I was excited. And I had never been more terrified in my life. I really didn't know what a truly healthy marriage looked like. One day during a time in prayer, I felt as if God showed me my fears: *What if we can't make it work? What if Duncan makes choices that break my heart?* It was at that moment that I chose to forgive anything and everything that would come our way.

In the midst of excruciating circumstances, I had to face my decision from that day head-on. Would I forgive the deep and painful breach of trust and intimacy that was now in front of me? I knew that choosing forgiveness in this moment meant that I had to live this choice out. Forgiveness was not merely a word. It was my word to Duncan that I would never use his actions as a weapon against him. Without forgiveness, he would be living in a never-ending cycle of punishment.

Is it cruel to suggest forgiveness as part of the healing process? Why should the wounded and victimized give this gift, especially to those who seemingly have no remorse for their actions? When we view forgiveness through this lens, we miss what it really is and is not.

Unforgiveness keeps us in bondage. Trapped in memories and flashbacks. Trying desperately to make sense of what we have endured. Locked in a tower, counting and recounting what was stolen from us. Tallying it up. Counting it again and again. While missing out on what counts today. Forgiveness is the gift that sets us free.

Forgive and forget is what God does. Forgive and entrust the memories and pain to God is our part. Forgiveness does not mean the memory goes away. It means the memory can no longer torment us. Forgiveness does not automatically imply heart healing, yet we cannot heal without forgiving. Forgiving someone does not deny the evil the person has done, nor does it remove the consequences he or she may face.

The point of forgiveness is not reconciliation. Reconciliation requires a person's changed behavior and the rebuilding of trust. And that is not something we control.

Forgiveness is trusting God to determine the judgment for another's actions. It frees us from carrying the weight of any person's sin. Forgiveness is a choice to release the sins against us, and place them in God's hands. Trusting that God can make all things right is the only way forward.

I have learned that what we do not release in forgiveness, we will repeat.

Sure, we may not do to others exactly what was done to us. But as unforgiveness remains and we stay focused on the injustice of it all, we will create a life that wounds others. I had to make a choice: Would I renounce or repeat the sins against me?

When I am hurting because of another's actions, it has helped me to focus on love. Who does *love* say this person is? What would *love* say to this person? We all move through the world, acting and reacting, often hurting those around us. We do not ignore bad behavior, or allow abuse. Boundaries are good and healthy. Hard conversations are a must. But we can begin to see and understand that the things people say and do to us are often a reflection of their own hurting, locked-away hearts. This perspective comes as we open our hearts to God. We will begin to see others as He sees them. We will see His longing to reach into their hearts with love.

We must, in our pain, learn to sit in love. Absorbing all of God's love for us, until it flows out of us to others. Whether or not you ever see or speak to that person again whom you're forgiving, you can still make forgiveness a regular practice. This is how we heal. By allowing love to wash the pain away, releasing those whose actions and words created the wounds.

The Torment of Unforgiveness

We will not heal by staying in a place of unforgiveness.

Choosing to forgive is an act of faith. We are entrusting our past, present, and future to God. Paul, in a letter to the church in Corinth, addresses a situation that he has been helping the people walk through. It sounds like a messy, painful, and outright wrong situation, and it was happening in the church!

Yet things seem to have moved toward healing and repentance. Paul writes, "When you forgive this man, I forgive him, too. And when I forgive whatever needs to be forgiven, I do so with Christ's authority for your benefit, so that Satan will not outsmart us. For we are familiar with his evil schemes" (2 Corinthians 2:10-11).

Forgiveness is how we overcome evil schemes. Lies, shame, fear, and repeating what was done to us are all disarmed as we release forgiveness toward those who have hurt us. This is how we overcome evil and darkness.

Unforgiveness opens *you* up to torment. Unforgiveness leaves *you* bound in what happened. Unforgiveness keeps *you* from receiving God's forgiveness and finding your healing. Forgiveness is a gift that sets us free to live and walk in love and wholeness.

Here is the really important part: When we refuse to forgive the actions of others against us, God will not forgive us our offenses. "If you forgive those who sin against you, your heavenly Father will forgive you. But if you refuse to forgive others, your Father will not forgive your sins," Jesus told us in Matthew 6:14–15.

What is so powerful that it could stop God's forgiveness from flowing to us? I think of sins as debts. Taking from another what we cannot pay for: gossip that destroys trust, a lie that breaks a reputation, angry words that open the door to fear, actions that steal peace or confidence. Really, any selfish act that takes from another what cannot be restored. These are evil actions that leave a path of destruction that cannot simply be undone.

When you choose to forgive, however, you are releasing a debt owed to you. It doesn't seem fair to release the debt, does it? To let the guilty go free? To just let them get away with it, while you're left with nothing?

Hear me: No one, no matter how hard they tried, or how much they wanted to, could ever give back what they took, or undo the destruction that they caused. Are you ready for the really unfair part? The only person being held captive by unforgiveness is *you*.

When you choose unforgiveness, you choose to live within a system where everyone must pay their debts, including you. God has offered us a system that is unthinkable. We can release the sins against us to Him, and trust that He will give perfect healing, restoration, and justice for everyone involved. We love the idea of being forgiven for our sins. It is harder to accept that God would want to forgive others who have caused us so much pain.

We receive forgiveness as a gift. We must also give this gift, with no strings attached.

Remember, these are impossible debts. A lifetime of doing the right thing will never restore what we cannot repay. Just as no person can restore what he or she stole from us.

When I was really hurting, my mind would follow this train of thought: *Duncan owes me. And BIG.*

But what? And how? *What could he do to really make things right?* I wondered. *What could he ever do to take away the wound, the shame, the fear, the insecurity I'm now wrestling with?*

What would be enough? The truth is, there wasn't any action, word, or compensation on this planet that Duncan could offer that would cure the wound. Instead, God offered to purchase the debt Duncan owed me—to pay it not only in full, but above and beyond. When we forgive, the debt another person owes us now belongs to God. In exchange, our hearts are fully, wholly restored.

God doesn't bring about forgiveness in any other way than the one He has already provided: Jesus Christ becoming sin for all, and releasing forgiveness to all who would receive it. God is not going to forgive us in a system of our own making. A system where we demand justice from those who hurt us—full payment and compensation, even when we know that the debt is an impossible one. If we want justice on our terms rather than the terms God has provided, then He will allow this. But then our sins will also be subject to the rules we have come up with—leaving us to pay the debts we have incurred, in full, impossible though they may be.

God's forgiveness for you is not earned or deserved. It cannot be paid back. Likewise, the forgiveness He asks you to offer others is not earned or deserved. He asks us to release the debts others owe us that cannot be paid back, just as He has forgiven the debts owed to Him that we could not pay.

> *We want justice, but we need healing. Healing does not come from everything being made right on our terms. Healing comes from releasing our pain to God...*

We want justice, but we need healing. Healing does not come from everything being made right on our terms. Healing comes from releasing our pain to God, trusting Him to restore all that was lost, bring good from evil, and make all new. We are not paid back, not refurbished or remodeled, but we are made new, whole and better than before.

Forgiveness is this powerful.

The profound truth about forgiveness is this: Jesus died on the cross for the sins of all. He became all sin, carried it to the cross, and forever overcame its power. What was done to you was done to Christ. He took on that sin, and He forgave it, just as He forgave you for all of your sins.

"Against you, and you alone, have I sinned; I have done what is evil in your sight. You will be proved right in what you say, and your judgment against me is just" (Psalm 51:4).

Refusing to forgive someone declares that what Jesus offers for the debt of sin is not enough, and you want nothing to do with what He offers in exchange for the sins against you, or your sins against God. You are saying that you will pay your own debts, and you expect others to do the same. Yet no one can pay this kind of debt.

Only God can restore what was taken from you. Not only does God restore, but by His Word, His life, and His love, He can create such an abundance that you end up with so much more than before. And certainly more than any person could have given you, even if that person gave you everything he or she had.

While there will be hard discussions and consequences resulting from people's actions, you choose to release others with grace and humility. You choose to see them as forgiven and clean from their sin. You have released their debt to you, and refuse to require any payment or compensation.

What Forgiveness Is *Not*

There are more misunderstandings that we can address about forgiveness. Here is what forgiveness is not:

- Forgiveness is not easy.

- Forgiveness is not a one-and-done process. I learned from reading Lysa TerKeurst's book *Forgiving What You Can't Forget* that it is normal and healthy to forgive in layers. We often need to forgive both the action *and* the impact of someone's choices. Impact is revealed over time, in layers, bit by bit. This doesn't mean that you haven't forgiven; it just means you are aware of another layer of impact that needs to be forgiven.

- Forgiveness does not mean that you must allow people back into your life who are still abusive or destructive. It is both/and. You can forgive *and* choose not to be in a relationship until real change occurs. You can forgive *and* set healthy boundaries.

- Forgiveness is not ignoring what was done, or pretending the pain is not real. Forgiveness is a step toward your own freedom and healing.

- Forgiveness does not assume reconciliation. A restored and healed relationship may not be possible. Where it is, both parties will need to work toward rebuilding trust, safety, and a healthy relationship.

- Forgiveness does not mean that what was done is brushed under the rug and can no longer be discussed or processed. You can forgive *and* still process what was done with a counselor or friend. And if possible, discuss it with the person being forgiven.

- Forgiveness does not take away the reality of what happened. It takes away the torment of being forever stuck in what happened. Forgiveness opens a path before you of freedom and healing.

The First Step Is Forgiveness

You can forgive *and* still be hurt and angry. The first step to being wholly, truly free is forgiveness. Not because the other person deserves it, but because you need it.

If you are struggling with this topic, please check out Lysa TerKeurst's book I just mentioned, *Forgiving What You Can't Forget*. I found it incredibly helpful and comforting.

I heard a message in the spring of 2020 by Kris Vallotton that held a key to healing our marriage. At the time, Covid was wreaking havoc and causing fear around the globe, and Kris's message to the church was simply this: *Humility is the way forward*. (You can listen to this amazing message for yourself at https://podcast.krisvallotton.com/humility-is-the-way-forward).

Our marriage was in a crisis of its own, and this word resonated deeply with me. Forgiveness requires humility. Restoration requires humility. Healing requires humility. Forgiveness reminds us that we, too, are capable of deeply wounding others in ways that we cannot restore.

As we were healing, I asked Duncan why he stayed in our marriage. His answer was, *Because you showed me real love.*

Doesn't that look great on paper?! The reality was much more difficult. I had to decide every day to pick up hope, to choose love, to take a big dose of humility, and to extend forgiveness. I had to set my eyes on Jesus when emotions and fears and pain were crashing around me, threatening to drag me into the depths. I didn't always get it right. Forgiveness didn't take away the pain. Forgiveness didn't make me forget. Forgiveness didn't instantly heal our relationship. But it gave us a chance.

I didn't choose love as a means to an end. Love was not a strategy to trick Duncan or manipulate him. Please do not hear the lessons I have poured out in these pages as strategies to manipulate the outcome you want. From the beginning, I knew that I could not be without Jesus, and in order to keep Him close, I could not harden my heart to love. This is what empowered me every day: *Please God, don't let my heart become hardened to your love.*

Remember the promise of the dimes? (See chapter 8 for a quick refresher.) Forgiveness allows you to receive a multiplication back of what was lost. Only God can do this. You can't demand it from those who owe you. You can't hold onto the debt others owe you and receive a multiplication from God.

When you release the debt owed to you, you choose to forgive what was done to you, stolen from you, and said about you. God will then release the debt you owe to Him. You step out of the loan-shark mentality, and into grace. We must have a firm grasp on this reality in order to extend it to others.

Has God graciously forgiven you? Then graciously forgive one another in the depths of Christ's love. Ephesians 4:32 TPT

- TWENTY-FIVE -
"Did You Learn to Love?"

Several years ago, I heard a woman tell her story of dying and seeing Jesus. She tells of being in His presence during this time, and having Him ask her, *Did you learn to love?* This question has resonated with me ever since. Out of all our pursuits, desires, and accomplishments on this earth, is our highest calling and purpose to *learn to love*? This woman was brought back to life with a new focus. I hope that in all of the pain and suffering, the joyous overcoming, and even the most mundane of chores, we, too, will see that our one focus is to *learn to love*.

In 1 John chapter 4, we read more than once that we are only capable of love because God first loved us. We are invited into a beautiful circle of receiving God's perfect love and releasing it to all we come into contact with:

> This is real love—not that we loved God, but that he loved us and sent his Son as a sacrifice to take away our sins. 1 John 4:10

> We love each other because he loved us first. 1 John 4:19

Facing the aftermath of Duncan's affair was beyond painful. There were days I truly thought I would never feel peace again. The mental and emotional torment was crushing.

In and through it all, love healed me—or rather, Love personified healed me. God Himself, the One who *is* Love, never left me:

> God is love, and all who live in love live in God, and God lives in them. 1 John 4:16

With Love by my side—in fact, with Love Himself actually living *inside* me—the trial sent to destroy me refined me. People will give us plenty of opportunities to lean into Love Himself, and to choose love over fear. As we lean into the One who is love, fear will lose its grip on us, and love will begin to flow out of us.

This book's purpose is not to save a marriage after infidelity, although that would be a beautiful outcome! I wrote this book to show you that healing and wholeness are possible, no matter what you have endured. As I faced the trials I've told you about in these pages, I knew it was not possible to hold onto pain and be close to Jesus. When we refuse to let go of Jesus, He will help us release all of the anger, fear, shame, and bitterness that is so tempting to hold onto. By choosing love over fear each day, we will drop the baggage and leave it behind forever.

Duncan and I have been more intentional in the last five years of our marriage than the first thirteen. Healing the pain of betrayal was not easy. Residue still clings to my soul, surprising me at times with fear and doubt to combat. Questions arise that lead to more conversations for Duncan and me to have. Yet with each step toward Jesus and healing, the questions have subsided. The triggers that would have taken me days to process now take hours, if not minutes, to acknowledge and address. What once felt irreparable and impossible to overcome no longer torments me.

I chose love, and the tools I presented to you in this book kept me in step with love. Duncan chose love, too. He chose to face himself, me, and God. He chose to rebuild trust. Our marriage survived the lies, betrayal, and pain because Duncan chose to turn toward me when I was hurting. Without both of our hearts coming toward each other with humility, grace, and truth, this outcome would not be our story.

"Are we okay?"

Ignoring Duncan's choices, or shoving the pain deep, deep down into my soul was not how our marriage survived. I did not pretend that nothing had happened. I did not slap on a fake smile and act as if I were fine. I chose forgiveness, which meant never using Duncan's choices as a weapon against him. I often stumbled over all the ways betrayal had impacted me. But I made the decision to continually release and forgive him in it all.

When I was struggling with the pain Duncan's actions caused, I let him know, fully and honestly. Without blame, or anger. It was more of a confession of what I was going through. Being able to release that to him helped heal my heart, and it allowed Duncan to show up for me in ways that helped heal our connection.

I started a phrase, unintentionally at first, as a way to check in with Duncan when I was afraid: *"Are we okay?"* After a handful of times of me asking him this, Duncan was frustrated: "Why do you keep asking that? I don't think we're okay, and I'm not sure this will ever be okay."

I took a minute to think about what I was asking and explained to him that in those moments, I needed to know if he was still in this with me—that he wanted to be here with me *and* fight for "us" together. Once he understood where the question was coming from, he changed his response. To this day, if I am feeling triggered, I can ask him, *"Are we okay?"* And he will pause whatever he is doing, wrap me in his arms, and tell me, "Oh yeah, we're good!"

It is truly a miracle that our marriage could not only survive this wound, but grow into more than either of us hoped for.

Jesus has conquered the storms that swirl around us and the waves that threaten to overtake us. Now, we, too, can walk through this life with confidence and power in every storm. His true and faithful love is the freedom and authority we need, no matter what life throws at us or what the outcome is.

Through prayer and forgiveness (and often repentance), I held on, though barely at times, to the hope that our marriage would heal, and would be better than ever.

My Testimony Can Be Yours . . .

This book is not a step-by-step guide for you as you overcome suffering. It is a compilation of what worked some days, and what worked others. I looked for Jesus and invited Him into every hurting place. I sought Him, no matter how things looked. I told Him when I was angry. I prayed bold, faith-filled prayers some days, and other days barely there whispers of *Jesus, help!* I wept. I screamed and cussed like a sailor. I broke my hand. I faced off with my demonic agreements and addressed the lies I was believing. At times, I could only break down helplessly and allow others to sing and pray over me. And in it all, humility was indeed the way forward.

> *My testimony is this: Jesus has set me free and made me whole.*

Jesus still does miracles today. The most beautiful ones are done deep within the human heart. My testimony is this: Jesus has set me free and made me whole. I learned to trust and forgive what seemed unforgivable. Jesus opened Duncan's eyes to truth and love. Jesus held two broken hearts together until they were again one.

Jesus is the path to wholeness and freedom. My testimony can become your testimony too. All the lies and snares of the trauma you have experienced—or are in the middle of right this very moment—can be completely unraveled.

The unraveling is a good thing. It may feel difficult along the way, or even impossible. I hope that in reading these pages, you have found the ability to hope, and to trust in the strong arm of the One who is Love. He will be there to lift you up. You won't go under in the storm! He is with you, weaving your life back together into something more amazing than you could ever imagine in the midst of your pain. He is setting you free and making you whole.

I pray that your heart will awaken to the beauty and power of God's love for you. Please, my friend, do not let your heart grow cold. God has a beautiful future ahead for you. Keep believing, keep hoping, and keep choosing love. One day, one step at a time, you will be whole again

- NOTES -

Front Pages

[1] Cambridge Dictionary, s.v. "be undone," https://dictionary.cambridge.org/us/dictionary/english/be-undone#google_vignette.
[2] Definition based on Cambridge Dictionary, s.v. "unstuck," https://dictionary.cambridge.org/us/dictionary/english/unstuck.
[3] Definition based on Merriam-Webster's Unabridged Dictionary, s.v. "unstuck," https://unabridged.merriam-webster.com/unabridged/unstuck.
[4] Definitions based on Merriam-Webster Dictionary, s.v. "unravel," accessed November 16, 2023, https://www.merriam-webster.com/dictionary/unravel.

Part One: becoming undone

[1] Cambridge Dictionary, s.v. "be undone," https://dictionary.cambridge.org/us/dictionary/english/be-undone#google_vignette.

Notes

Chapter Three: Lost Hearts

1. Blue Letter Bible, s.v. "faint" (Strong's G1590), https://www.blueletterbible.org/search/Dictionary/viewTopic.cfm?topic=VT0000984#vineDiv.

Chapter Six: The Weapons We Love With

1. These bullet points are from verses 4–6 of 1 Corinthians 13 (NLT).

Chapter Seven: The Battle for Your Future

1. Merriam-Webster Dictionary, s.v. "deem," https://www.merriam-webster.com/dictionary/deem.

Chapter Eight: Dusty Trails and Messy Rivers

1. See Proverbs 6:30–31.

Chapter Nine: The Reasons We Stay Broken

1. Note that the Amplified Bible quotations in this chapter are taken from the Classic Edition (AMPC).

Part Two: becoming unstuck

1. Definition based on Cambridge Dictionary, s.v. "unstuck," https://dictionary.cambridge.org/us/dictionary/english/unstuck.
2. Definition based on Merriam-Webster's Unabridged Dictionary, s.v. "unstuck," https://unabridged.merriam-webster.com/unabridged/unstuck.

Chapter Eleven: How Stories Are Written

[1] This is my paraphrase of Proverbs 17:19, but see it in The Message translation.

Chapter Twelve: At the Crossroads

[1] Blue Letter Bible, s.v. "ḥārān" (Strong's H2771), citing the Assyrian word ḥarrânu, https://www.blueletterbible.org/lexicon/h2771/kjv/wlc/0-1/.

Chapter Thirteen: Purpose in the Pain

[1] Israeli artist Yehuda Bacon, who survived the Holocaust, said this, as quoted in Viktor E. Frankl, The Will to Meaning: Foundations and Applications of Logotherapy (New York: Penguin Group, 2014), 57.
[2] Bessel A. van der Kolk, M.D., The Body Keeps the Score: Brain, Mind, and Body in the Healing of Trauma (New York, Penguin Books, 2014), 17.

Chapter Fourteen: "Why, God?"

[1] See also Joshua 1:5, where God says to Joshua (and to us), "As I was with Moses, so I will be with you; I will not fail you or forsake you."

Chapter Fifteen: Overcoming Doubt

[1] For more on this idea, see page 28 of Ray McAllister, "Theology of Blindness in the Hebrew Scriptures," Andrews University Digital Library of Dissertations and Theses, May 2010, https://digitalcommons.andrews.edu/cgi/viewcontent.cgi?article=1088&context=dissertation.

[2] Blue Letter Bible, s.v. "alla" (Strong's G235), https://www.blueletterbible.org/lexicon/g235/kjv/tr/0-1/.
[3] Ibid.

Chapter Sixteen: Emotions Are Good

[1] See the "Etymology" section at Merriam-Webster Dictionary, s.v. "sympathy," https://www.merriam-webster.com/dictionary/sympathy.

Chapter Seventeen: Being Human

[1] Blue Letter Bible, s.v. "šāḇar" (Strong's H7665), https://www.blueletterbible.org/lexicon/h7665/kjv/wlc/0-1/.
[2] Blue Letter Bible, s.v. "lēḇ" (Strong's H3820), https://www.blueletterbible.org/lexicon/h3820/kjv/wlc/0-1/.

Part Three: becoming unraveled

[1] Definitions based on Merriam-Webster Dictionary, s.v. "unravel," accessed November 16, 2023, https://www.merriam-webster.com/dictionary/unravel.

Chapter Eighteen: Light & Water

[1] The Scripture quotations from Psalm 18 are taken from The Passion Translation of the Bible (TPT).

Chapter Twenty-Three: Fire Forged

[1] Blue Letter Bible, s.v. "synergeō" (Strong's G4903), https://www.blueletterbible.org/lexicon/g4903/kjv/tr/0-1/.

²See Numbers 23:19.
³Bible Tools, s.v. "hupomonē" (Strong's G5281), https://www.bibletools.org/index.cfm/fuseaction/Lexicon.show/ID/G5281/hupomone.htm.

About the Author

Annie Callahan is passionate about empowering others to grow in life and business through the timeless wisdom of the Bible. She preaches and teaches the Bible, helping people find freedom, embrace their calling, and experience transformation through God's Word. Residing in the beautiful Colorado mountains with her husband and daughters, Annie is dedicated to equipping others for their journey of faith and purpose.

Connect with Annie:

Website: anniecallahan.com
Instagram: @anniecallahan_speaks
Facebook: @anniecallahanspeaks